NEW TESTAMENT AND SEPTUAGINT

BY

ALEXANDER SPERBER

Jewish Theological Seminary of America

WIPF & STOCK · Eugene, Oregon

Reprinted from the Journal of Biblical Literature,
Vol. LIX, Part II, pp. 193–293.

Wipf and Stock Publishers
199 W 8th Ave, Suite 3
Eugene, OR 97401

New Testament and Septuagint
By Sperber, Alexander
Softcover ISBN-13: 978-1-7252-8042-7
Publication date 5/7/2020
Previously published by SBL, 1940

To the memory of
DOCTOR CYRUS ADLER

TABLE OF CONTENTS

A. THE PROBLEM: pp. 193–205.
    I. The OT and the Christian Mission.— II. OT and NT combined form the Bible of the Church.— III. OT quotations in the NT.— IV. Previous Researches.— V. The Problem.

B. ORIGEN'S HEXAPLA: pp. 205–248.
    VI. Lagarde's Archetype theory.— VII. The current view on Origen's work.— VIII. Refutation thereof.— IX. A new approach.— X. The Septuagint according to the Hexapla.— XI. The Hebrew Bible according to the Hexapla.

C. THE OLDEST MANUSCRIPTS OF THE BIBLE IN GREEK: pp. 248–266.
    XII. Codices B and A on the Pentateuch.— XIII. Codices B and A on Judges.— XIV. Codices B and A on the Bible.

D. THE CHURCH FATHERS AND VETUS LATINA: pp. 267–278.
    XV. The Minor Prophets in Greek.— XVI. The LXX in Latin.

E. CONCLUSIONS: pp. 278–289.
    XVII. The NT and the two LXX types.— XVIII. The final redaction of the Hebrew Bible.

INDEX OF BIBLICAL PASSAGES: pp. 290–293.

NEW TESTAMENT AND SEPTUAGINT

ALEXANDER SPERBER

JEWISH THEOLOGICAL SEMINARY

A. THE PROBLEM*

I. THE OLD TESTAMENT AND THE CHRISTIAN MISSION

IN THE first volume of his monumental work *The Expansion of Christianity in the first three centuries* (New York 1904), Adolf von Harnack devotes a full chapter to the discussion of the role, which the OT played in the propagation of Christianity during the first three centuries of the new era (p. 353). "The OT did exert an influence which brought it (scil. Christianity) to the verge of becoming the religion of a book" (p. 353). It overshadowed even the NT in importance; for "The NT as a whole did not generally play the same role as the OT in the mission and practice of the church" (p. 363).

If we ask for the reason why the OT was kept in so high a regard, we are told: "The OT certainly was a mighty help to the Christian propaganda, and it was in vain that the Jews protested. We have also one positive testimony, in the following passage from Tatian (Orat. XXIX.), that for many people *the OT formed the real bridge by which they crossed to Christianity*: 'Some barbarian writings came into my hands, which were too old for

---

*The following abbreviations are being used in this study: MT = Masoretic Text; SAM = Hebrew Pentateuch of the Samaritans; G = Septuagint according to codex B or, where missing, codex A; al ex = *alia exemplaria*, cf. X, § 1; Th = Theodoret of Kyros; Cy = Cyril of Alexandria; TRL = A. Sperber, "Hebrew based upon Greek and Latin Transliterations," *HUCA*, XII–XIII, Cincinnati 1938; HPT = A. Sperber, "Hebrew based upon Biblical Passages in Parallel Transmission," *HUCA*, XIV, Cincinnati 1939.

Greek ideas and too divine for Greek errors. *These I was led to trust, owing to . . . . their foreknowledge of the future'* " (p. 355). Tatian thus admits that, while reading the OT, he became converted to Christianity, since there he found events forestalled which later on actually happened. The necessity of regularly reading in the OT was emphasized by the early Church. See Origen's statement (*Hom. II in Num.*; X, p. 19) that two hours of daily Bible reading could hardly be regarded as sufficient. This and other pertinent passages in Origen's works are indicated in Harnack's *Bible Reading*, 69, note 1. They led Harnack to the following conclusion: "From the OT it could be proved that the appearance and the entire history of Jesus had been previously predicted hundreds and even thousands of years ago; and further, that the founding of the New People which was to be fashioned out of all nations upon earth, had from the very beginning been prophesied and prepared for. *Their own religion appeared, on the basis of this book, to be the religion of a history which was the fulfilment of prophecy*" (pp. 358 f.).

In other words, the missionary preachers, who went out in those early centuries to spread Christianity, believed for themselves and likewise impressed their audiences that they were not teaching a new religion, but that they were conveying the message of the final fulfillment of certain ancient prophecies made to the Hebrews. The NT itself reflects this attitude. When Paul, accompanied by Silas, arrived at Thessalonica, he preached there in the Synagogue, "and three Sabbath days *reasoned with them out of the Scriptures*, opening and alleging, *that Christ must needs have suffered and risen again from the dead*; and that this Jesus, whom I preach unto you, is Christ" (Acts 17 2–3). This procedure was by no means an exceptional one, related for its uniqueness; on the contrary, the introductory phrase "And Paul, *as his manner was*, went in unto them" (Acts 17 2) shows that this was sheer routine with Paul. The very fact that Paul took pains in order to prove from the Scriptures that his was a message of fulfillment, shows that these Scriptures must have been widely known among his listeners. This assumption is corroborated by an express statement, referring to the Jewish population of Beroea, which upon hearing Paul's exegesis "searched the Scriptures daily, whether those things were so" (Acts 17 11). The emphasis which the early church thus laid upon its being a religion of fulfillment resulted in stressing the necessity that every Christian acquaint himself thoroughly with the Scriptures. Thus the OT gained wide circulation outside the Jewish communities. Harnack dealt with this particular aspect of early Christian mission among the heathen population in his monograph *Bible Reading in the Early Church* (New York, 1912). "At first primitive Christianity was concerned exclusively with the Scriptures of the *Old* Testament. Even the apologists, when speaking of Scriptures, mean only them" (p. 40, note 1). "The famous passage in the Epistle of Ignatius to the Philadelphians (chap. VIII.): "I have heard some say: *'If I do not find it in the Old Testament I do not believe it in the Gospel'* "— presupposes laymen who knew the Scriptures" (p. 40). "Aristides, the earliest of the apologists, exhorts his heathen readers, after reading his own work to take into their hands and to read the Holy Scriptures themselves. This appeal to the Holy Scriptures runs through all the apologies from the earliest to the latest, and shows that their authors were united in the belief that *the regular way to become a convinced Christian was to read the Holy Scriptures*. In this way Justin, Tatian, and Theophilus expressly say that they themselves became Christians" (p. 42 f.).

II. THE OLD AND NEW TESTAMENT COMBINED FORM THE BIBLE OF THE CHURCH.

On the basis of these statements we may well assume that the missionaries, who set forth to preach the Gospel of Christianity, took along with them a Bible to prove the authenticity of their message. This Bible, which originally consisted of the OT alone, was afterwards extended to include the books of the NT (cf. *Bible Reading*, p. 40, note 1). Thus, finally, the Bible of the Church was complete: it presented the prophecy of the OT, and its fulfillment in the NT. In order to appeal to the prospective Christians and to the newly made converts of heathen origin, both Testaments had to be presented to them in Greek. Whether the Greek of the NT is genuine or a mere translation from an Aramaic original, does not matter in this connection; (the OT in Greek no doubt was merely a translation and still the prophecies contained therein were considered authoritative nevertheless); just the same, no English churchgoer worries over the fact that his Bible after all is only a translation from the Hebrew or Greek. For he turns to his Bible for religious and not for linguistic reasons. And religion he is sure to find here, the same as the early convert to Christianity found in the two parts of his Bible, according to the statements cited above, the prophecy and account of the coming of the Christ.

This procedure of combining the OT and NT into one complete Bible was early adopted by the Church and then retained throughout the centuries. We note, therefore, that even the oldest manuscripts of the Bible in Greek conform with this rule.

III. Old Testament Quotations in the New Testament.

Thus LXX and NT form a unity, the Bible. And with the statements of Tatian and other early Christian writers, referring to their interrelation as prophecy and fulfillment — as cited above — in mind, we may now attempt to verify some messages of fulfillment as narrated in the NT, on the basis of the pertinent prophecies of the OT. To this end we shall refer in our quotations to the readings of Codex B for both the OT and NT. This Manuscript is admittedly the oldest text-witness which contains almost the entire Bible. Our examination will prove whether or not the underlying text represents a unity.

a. Quotations in the Gospels

1. In Matth 2 4–6 the incident of the visit of the three wise men is told, which caused Herod considerable embarrassment. The experts whom he consulted told him that the Messiah was to be born in Bethlehem in Juda, and quoted: και συ βηθλεεμ γη ιουδα, ουδαμως ελαχιστη ει εν τοις ηγεμοσιν ιουδα· εκ σου γαρ εξελευσεται ηγουμενος, οστις ποιμανει τον λαον μου ισραηλ. This clearly is a reference to Micah 5 1, which

reads in the OT section of the very same Bible Ms. B as follows: και συ βηθλεεμ οικος εφραθα, ολιγοστος ει του ειναι εν χιλιασιν ιουδα · εξ ου μοι εξελευσεται του ειναι εις αρχοντα του ισραηλ. We are not concerned with the explanation of minor discrepancies: such as εξ ου and εκ σου, where the first is merely a phonetic confusion of the latter; or that ηγεμοσιν and χιλιασιν reflect two different etymologic derivations of the consonants of one and the same basic Hebrew word באלפי, pronounced as בְּאַלְפֵי or בְּאָלְפֵי respectively, which in itself proves that the NT quotation and the LXX on this passage both go back to two independent translations of this verse in Hebrew into Greek (cf. *JBL*, 1935, 82, paragraph II for similar cases). But quite apart from this we wish to stress the point that the verse in the LXX is entirely different from the one quoted by Matthew; moreover: a reading βηθλεεμ οικος εφραθα could never have been considered as a prophecy for βηθλεεμ της ιουδαιας. The incongruity is too obvious.

2. We continue with Matthew's report. The Virgin Mary with the infant Jesus had to flee to Egypt for their lives, according to a vision which Joseph had. They remained there until the death of Herod, and the whole incident was predetermined by the necessity to fulfill the prophetic statement εξ αιγυπτου εκαλεσα τον υιον μου (verses 14–15). Hence Herod was not acting of his own free evil intention, but was merely an instrument in the hands of the Lord, so that things should happen, which had to happen. We now turn to Hos 11 1, again in the same Bible manuscript B, in anticipation of finding here the prophecy: οτι νηπιος ισραηλ και εγω ηγαπησα αυτον, και εξ αιγυπτου μετεκαλεσα τα τεκνα αυτου. Here τα τεκνα αυτου, his children, clearly refers to ισραηλ mentioned at the beginning of the verse, and no exegesis could twist it round to mean τον υιον μου, one person out of the multitude of the Israelites, who was in addition *the* son of the Lord.

3. The flight to Egypt infuriated Herod; he took his revenge by killing the innocent infants left in Bethlehem. And even this atrocity was foreseen long ago by Jeremiah in the statement: φωνη εν ραμα ηκουσθη, κλαυθμος και οδυρμος πολυς · ραχηλ κλαιουσα τα τεκνα αυτης, και ουκ ηθελεν παρακληθηναι,

οτι ουκ εισιν. (verses 17-18). But in Jer 31 15 this passage reads: φωνη εν ραμα ηκουσθη, θρηνου και κλαυθμου και οδυρμου· ραχηλ αποκλαιομενη ουκ ηθελεν παυσασθαι επι τοις υιοις αυτης, οτι ουκ εισιν. The passage in Matthew is represented as being a quotation; but though this verse in Matthew shows a great resemblance to that in Jeremiah, it can in no way be considered a direct citation.

4. The great similarity between this Jeremiah verse in the OT section of Codex B and the way it is quoted in the NT part of that Manuscript might lead to an explanation that Matthew at least in this particular case deliberately changed the exact wording of his original, namely the LXX, in order to improve on the Greek style or diction of the passage. But any attempt to explain away in such a fashion the apparent differences between the two sections of the Bible in Greek must end in a complete failure. One more instance, taken from Matthew again, will suffice to clarify this issue: In his record on Jesus healing the sick and obsessed ones on the Sabbath day, in chapter 12, Matthew remarks that these things had to happen again to fulfill the prophecy: ιδου ο παις· μου, ον ηρετισα, ο αγαπητος μου, εις ον ευδοκησεν η ψυχη μου· θησω το πνευμα μου επ αυτον, και κρισιν τοις εθνεσιν απαγγελει· ουκ ερισει ουδε κραυγασει, ουδε ακουει τις εν ταις πλατειαις την φωνην αυτου· καλαμον συντετριμμενον ου κατεαξει και λινον τυφομενον ου σβεσει, εως αν εκβαλη εις νικος την κρισιν· και τω ονοματι αυτου εθνη ελπιουσιν. (verses 17-21). It is quite enough to put the corresponding verses Is 42 1-4 of the LXX in juxtaposition, in order to be convinced that they cannot be regarded as the original of this quotation: ιακωβ ο παις μου, αντιλημψομαι αυτου· ισραηλ ο εκλεκτος μου, προσεδεξατο αυτον η ψυχη μου· εδωκα το πνευμα μου επ αυτον, κρισιν τοις εθνεσιν εξοισει· ου κεκραξεται ουδε ανησει ουδε ακουσθησεται εξω η φωνη αυτου· καλαμον τεθλασμενον ου συντριψει, και λινον καπνιζομενον ου σβεσει, αλλα εις αληθειαν εξοισει κρισιν· και επι τω ονοματι αυτου εθνη ελπιουσιν. It is quite impossible to regard these two ways of rendering the Hebrew text of Is 42 1-4 into Greek as interdependent; the differences are too many and they inter-

fere in too great a measure with the very structure of the sentences. But, above all other considerations, in the LXX the terms παις and εκλεκτος plainly mean the people of Israel as such, which is referred to by the words ιακωβ and ισραηλ, respectively. How, then, could Matthew see therein an anticipation of Jesus' appearance, thus inferring that Isaiah foresaw his coming and called him "son" and "beloved" of the Lord, and that by this divine providence Jesus was bound to act the way he did, in order to fulfill the words of the prophet? We would consider it poor method to say that Matthew overlooked the references to ιακωβ and ισραηλ, or even — and this would be much worse — purposely suppressed them. *One can not base a theology upon misquotations*! Consequently, there can be no thought of interdependence between the LXX rendering of these verses and their quotation by Matthew.

5. In order to round up the picture of the life history of Jesus seen as the history of fulfillment, we turn to John for the narrative of the very last incident in his earthly career: Jesus on the cross. For John says that the legs of Jesus were not broken, but his side was pierced by a spear, in order to fulfill the two prophecies: οστουν ου συντριβησεται αυτου, and οψονται εις ον εξεκεντησαν (19 32–37). The first reference is to Ex 12 46; but this verse reads in the LXX: και οστουν ου συντριψετε απ αυτου. The active construction of the verb makes this verse an ordinance for the Israelites, telling them what they are forbidden to do, while the passive construction in John turns the sentence round to say: what shall not be done to him. Important as the difference in meaning undoubtedly is, it looks insignificant when compared with the second reference to the Scriptures, namely Zech 12 10, which reads in the Septuagint: και επιβλεψονται προς με ανθ ων κατωρχησαντο. This translation is the result of the LXX's mistakenly reading the Hebrew דקרו as רקדו (metathesis, cf. *HPT*, § 36). According to John, the Roman soldier transfixed Jesus with his spear, in order to fulfill an ancient prophecy; εξεκεντησαν is a most suitable expression, indeed, to describe this action. But the corresponding κατωρχησαντο in the LXX indicates "to dance." All the favorite explanations of such discrepancies, that they

are free citations, reflect bad memory, etc., fall short of explaining an assumption that John while reading in his OT κατωρχησαντο, was reminded of the episode of the crucifixion, and quoted the passage as εξεκεντησαν.

b. Classification of the Differences

I hope that these few examples are convincing enough to demonstrate the problem in all its boldness. For a more detailed treatment I must refer to my article "The New Testament and the Septuagint," which appeared in the Hebrew Quarterly *Tarbiz*, Jerusalem, VI (1934), 1–29. For the benefit of those interested in the subject, but who are not sufficiently conversant with Hebrew to make free use of that article, I must give here a brief description of its contents. I first went carefully through the entire NT in Greek according to Nestle's editions, which is based upon Codex B, and excerpted all those passages, which are direct quotations from the OT, without paying attention to whether or not an introductory phrase like γεγραπται, η γραφη λεγει, το ρηϑεν indicates these passages to be direct quotations. For even in the event of the absence of such a phrase, they definitely go back to the OT and prove to what an extent the speech and thought of the authors of the NT were under the spell of the OT text. The relation of the language of mediaeval Hebrew works (such as שבט יהודה) to that of the Hebrew Bible is not too far fetched a comparison.

This material, which emanates, as I said, from the NT according to Codex B, I then compared with the respective OT passages in Greek in that very same Codex B; after eliminating those instances which I found in full agreement between the NT and OT sections of Codex B, there still remained approximately three hundred passages which appear as quotations in the NT in a wording more or less different from that found in their original places in the OT. With an eye on the basic Hebrew text I tried to group and classify these variants according to the following criteria: I. Greek synonyms. II. Differences in the exegesis of the same basic Hebrew word. III. The use of the possessive pronoun. IV. *Waw conjunctivum* in Greek translation. V. The use of the personal pronoun. VI. The use of the article. VII. Collective nouns treated as singulars or plurals. VIII. Verb and compound. IX. The use of the Greek tenses and modes. X. Differences in Greek syntax. XI. Addition or omission of Greek particles. XII. Hebrew particles in Greek translation. XIII. Different interpretation of full sentences. XIV. Inner Greek corruptions. XV. Differences resulting from Hebrew *variae lectiones*.

c. These Differences are of Theological Importance

While going through this enumeration of headings, under which the entire material could be listed, the reader might feel doubtful as to whether so strictly linguistic a method is appropriate to the theological nature of the texts involved. For the apostles, one might argue, were primarily concerned to prove their theological ideas, and one should not expect them to pay more than average attention to matters of diction and style. The best refutation of such an objection is to illustrate my procedure by way of examples: Paragraph IV deals with the rendering of Hebrew conjunctive *waw* into the Greek και or η. Both reflect the respective meaning of this particle in its various connections. When we read in Ex 21 15, ומכה אביו ואמו, or ib. verse 17: ומקלל אביו ואמו, it is obvious that the *waw* in ואמו means "or." But when we find Hos 6 6: כי חסד חפצתי ולא זבח translated in the LXX διοτι ελεος θελω η θυσιαν, while in Mat 9 13, and 12 7 the verse is quoted as ελεος θελω και ου θυσιαν, this difference και — η becomes highly significant. According to the conception of the LXX, the Lord merely *prefers* ελεος to sacrifice; this certainly does not exclude the sacrifice as a means to please the Lord, though it is less pleasing than ελεος. But the wording of Matthew plainly *rejects* the sacrifice: What the Lord wants is ελεος *and not sacrifice*!

Paragraph XI lists cases, where particles or similar parts of the speech are added or omitted. So in the case of Isa 28 16, המאמין לא יחיש, which the LXX translates και ο πιστευων ου μη καταισχυνθη: this is quoted in I Peter 2 6 and, with here unimportant variants, in Rom 9 33 as και ο πιστευων επ αυτω ου μη καταισχυνθη. Not belief general, but *belief in Jesus as the Christ*, is what Peter preaches: οτι χρηστος ο κυριος, προς ον προσερχομενοι, λιθον ζωντα.... παρα δε θεω εκλεκτον εντιμον, και αυτοι ως λιθοι ζωντες ... ανενεγκαι πνευματικας θυσιας ευπροσδεκτους θεω δια ιησου χριστου, διοτι περιεχει εν γραφη. ιδου τιθημι εν σιων λιθον ακρογωνιαιον εκλεκτον εντιμον, και ο πιστευων επ αυτω ου μη καταισχυνθη (verses 3–6). From the point of view of the grammarian, the words επ αυτω represent an addition as compared with the basic Hebrew text, and, therefore, are duly listed in paragraph XI (cf. now similarly *HPT*, § 124b 1). But there can be no doubt that Peter found this addition already in the OT in Greek at his disposal, and that he made bona fide theological use of it. It would be too absurd to suspect him of having changed the plain reading of the LXX text by such an insertion, and to base afterwards an entire theology upon this emended text of his own making!

I hope that these two examples are convincing enough and will dispell any such methodological objection as is indicated above.

The result of my examination of the OT quotations in the NT and the respective readings of the LXX section of the same Codex B proves that at as early a period as the time of the compilation of the NT, the OT in Greek must have been published and known in at least two forms, one known to us as the LXX, the other preserved to us in some, at least, of the quotations contained in the NT.

d. Jerome was aware of these difficulties

The apparent discrepancy between some of the OT quotations in the NT and the respective readings of the LXX was noticed in the early Church. Jerome justifies his method of basing his Latin translation upon the Hebrew text and not upon the LXX, though the latter enjoyed great authority as *the* Bible of the Church, by saying: "Quod ut auderem, Origenis me studium provocavit ... maximeque Evangelistarum et Apostolorum auctoritas, in quibus multa de veteri testamento legimus, quae in nostris codicibus [scil. of the LXX] non habentur."

(*Biblia Sacra iuxta Latinam Vulgatam versionem, Librum Genesis
... recensuit* D. Henricus Quentin, Romae, 1926. Sancti
Hieronymi Presbyteri Praefatio in Pentateuchum, p. 64). But
how are we to explain this fact? Did the authors of the NT
know of the LXX, and for some reason or other not consider it authoritative enough to be referred to, or were they in
ignorance of the very existence of this Greek Version of the
OT? Here Jerome is quite positive in his statement: "certe
apostoli et evangelistae Septuaginta interpretes noverant"
(Praefatio to Chronicles). If this be the case, so we must assume
that the authors of the NT had some good reason for deviating
from the LXX. Did they arbitrarily revise the text of such
passages, where they differ from the LXX, or had they a
Greek OT translation at their disposal, which actually contained the passages in question exactly in the same wording as
they quoted them? And if so, to which textual form of the OT
in Greek shall we give the preference: to the LXX or to those
manuscripts, of which the authors of the NT made use? This
is, what Jerome has to say on these questions: "sed et evangelistae et dominus quoque noster atque salvator nec non et Paulus
apostolus multa quasi de veteri testamento proferunt, quae in
nostris codicibus [scil. of the LXX] non habentur; super quibus
in suis locis plenius disseremus, ex quo perspicuum est illa magis
vera esse exemplaria, quae cum novi testamenti auctoritate
concordant" (*Quaestiones hebraicae in libro Geneseos*, ed. Paul
de Lagarde, Lipsiae 1868, 2 f.). From this statement we learn
that in Jerome's days there were still manuscripts of the OT in
Greek in existence which offered at the respective places a
textual form identical with that in which they appear in NT
quotations. No wonder that Jerome is inclined to attribute
greater authority to these codices, for the very reason that they
uphold the trustworthiness of the NT.

IV. Previous Researches in this Field.

H. B. Swete in his *Introduction to the Old Testament in Greek*
(Cambridge 1900), gives the following account of the relation,
which the NT quotations bear to the Alexandrian version (scil.

the LXX). "It may at once be said that every part of the New Testament affords evidence of a knowledge of the Septuagint, and that a great majority of the passages cited from the Old Testament are in general agreement with the Greek version. It is calculated by one writer on the subject (Turpie, *The old Testament in the New*, London 1868, 267) that . . . it departs from the Septuagint in 185 citations; and by another (Grinfield, *Apology for the Septuagint*, 1841, 37) that not more than fifty of the citations materially differ from the Septuagint. On either estimate the Septuagint is the principal source from which the writers of the New Testament derived their Old Testament quotations" (p. 392). "It is necessary to distinguish carefully between the causes which have produced variation. It may be due to (a) loose citation, or to (b) the substitution of a gloss for the precise words which the writer professes to quote, or to (c) a desire to adapt a prophetic context to the circumstances under which it was thought to have been fulfilled, or to (d) the fusing together of passages drawn from different contexts" (p. 394). After a discussion of five passages in Matthew, one of which is 2 6 (cf. above III a 1), Swete arrives at the conclusion that "the compiler of the first Gospel has more or less distinctly thrown off the yoke of the Alexandrian version and substituted for it a paraphrase, or an independent rendering from the Hebrew. But our evidence does not encourage the belief that the evangelist used or knew another complete Greek version of the Old Testament or of any particular book" (p. 398).

I hope that on the basis of my preceding expositions I may say that Swete was far from realizing the problem as such, and that all his remarks are consequently to be put into the discard.

V. The Problem.

Now that a translation of OT in Greek, distinct from the LXX, has appeared likely to have existed as the source of Biblical quotations in the NT, a work we may call the "Bible of the Apostles," the object of the present study is to find what of it we can identify. By the term "Bible of the Apostles" we don't mean to imply that the OT in Greek, which the respective authors or compilers of the entire NT used either as a basis for their narratives of events, or while expounding their theology, was a uniform textual type, so that all OT references therein could be made use of in our endeavors to reconstruct this Bible. We shall concern ourselves exclusively with the problem of the source or sources of those OT quotations, which are at a variance with their corresponding LXX passage. This textual type of the OT in Greek, whence they probably were taken, and of the nature of which for the time being we still know nothing, we call "Bible of the Apostles." The term is introduced here merely for practical purposes, to serve as a common denominator for the deviations from the LXX text.

B. ORIGEN'S HEXAPLA

VI. Lagarde's Archetype Theory.

In our search for the Bible of the Apostles we start with a re-examination of those facts concerning the OT in Greek which seem to be well established and are, therefore, generally agreed upon: we mean the LXX.

During the last sixty years, LXX studies were most deeply influenced by the theories of Paul de Lagarde, which in their turn were based on the following statement of Jerome in his *Praefatio* to Chronicles: "Nunc vero, cum pro varietate regionum diversa ferantur exemplaria ... Alexandria et Aegyptus in Septuaginta suis Hesychium laudat auctorem; Constantinopolis usque Antiochiam Luciani martyris exemplaria probat. Mediae inter has provinciae Palaestinos codices legunt, quos ab Origene elaboratos Eusebius et Pamphilius vulgaverunt; totusque orbis hac inter se trifaria varietate compugnat." According to the interpretation of Lagarde, this passage does not indicate that Origen, Lucian, and Hesychius were really "auctores" of respective new translations of the OT; to him they were merely revisers of the one existing text, the LXX, transforming it by additions, omissions or stylistic changes. I have dealt with this "Archetype" theory of Lagarde, and with the editions of texts by Lagarde and Rahlfs, respectively, which are based thereon, in my *Septuagintaprobleme* (Stuttgart, 1929) and in two papers, "The Problems of the Septuagint Recensions" (*JBL*, 1935, 73–92) and "Probleme einer Edition der Septuaginta" (*Festschrift Paul Kahle*, Leiden, 1935, 39–46). I hope I may say that I have refuted both, the basic theory and the subsequent text editions. I could also prove that Lucian and Hesychius represent two independent translations of the Hebrew Bible into Greek, and not two Greek recensions of one and the same translation according to Lagarde's theory.

Later on we shall have to refer to these results again. But now we wish to turn to Origen and his work. For since Origen ranks first among the three "auctores" whom Jerome mentions, from the point of view of mere chronology his work is of great importance.

VII. THE CURRENT VIEW ON ORIGEN'S WORK.

For a summary of the current view on this matter we turn again to H. B. Swete's *Introduction*; for A. Rahlfs, in his survey "History of the Septuagint Text," pp. XXII-XXXI of his *Septuaginta* (Stuttgart 1935), gives merely an abstract thereof, though he does not indicate Swete as his source. We shall, therefore, quote Swete's pertinent statements verbatim: "Between the years 220 and 250 he gave to the world a succession of commentaries, homilies or notes on nearly all the books of the Old Testament. In the course of these labours, perhaps from the moment that he began to read the Old Testament in the original, he was impressed with the importance of providing the Church with materials for ascertaining the true text and meaning of the original" (p. 60). "To attempt a new version was impracticable. It may be doubted whether Origen possessed the requisite knowledge of Hebrew ... On the other hand, Origen held that Christians must be taught frankly to recognize the divergences between the Septuagint and the current Hebrew text, and the superiority of Aquila and the other later versions, in so far as they were more faithful to the original; it was unfair to the Jew to quote against him passages from the Septuagint, which were wanting in his own Bible, and injurious to the Church herself to withhold from her anything in the Hebrew Bible which the Septuagint did not represent. Acting under these convictions Origen's first step was to collect all existing Greek versions of the Old Testament. He then proceeded to transcribe the versions in parallel columns, and to indicate in the column devoted to the Septuagint the relation in which the old Alexandrian version stood to the current Hebrew text" (p. 61). "The problem before him was to restore the Septuagint to its original purity, i. e. to the Hebraica veritas" (p. 68). "The additions and omissions in the Septuagint presented greater difficulty. Origen was unwilling to remove the former, for they belonged to the version which the Church had sanctioned, and which many Christians regarded as inspired Scripture; but he was equally unwilling to leave them without some mark of editorial disapprobation. Omissions were readily supplied from one of the other versions, namely Aquila or Theodotion, but the new matter interpolated into the Septuagint needed to be carefully distinguished from the genuine work of the Alexandrian translators. Here the genius of Origen found an ally in the system of critical signs which had its origin among the older scholars of Alexandria" (p. 69). "As employed by Origen in the fifth column of the Hexapla, the obelus was prefixed to words or lines which were wanting in the Hebrew, and therefore, from Origen's point of view, of doubtful authority, whilst the asterisk called attention to words or lines wanting in the Septuagint, but present in the Hebrew" (p. 70).

Jerome's explanation of the nature of Origen's work is somewhat different: "Origenis me studium provocavit, qui editioni antiquae translationem Theodotionis miscuit, asterisco et obelo, id est stella et veru, opus omne distinguens, dum aut inlucescere facit quae minus ante fuerat, aut superflua, quaeque iugulat et confodit" (*Praefatio in Pentateuchum*).

Thus Swete (with ample references from statements found in

early works on the subject) and Jerome agree in their definition of the Hexaplaric signs: asterisk signifying an addition, obelus an omission, in the basic text used for comparison. The basic text was Theodotion's version according to Jerome, but was the Hebrew Bible according to Swete, or rather according to the authorities whom he follows.

VIII. REFUTATION OF THE CURRENT VIEW.

The weak points of this approach to the problem are so obvious that one wonders how they remained unnoticed: 1. The LXX is a translation of the Hebrew Bible into Greek and, like all other ancient translations, no doubt follows slavishly the Hebrew original. If the divergences between the LXX and the Hebrew text as current in the days of Origen were so great and of such importance that "it was unfair to the Jew to quote him passages from the LXX, which were wanting in his own Bible, and injurious to the Church herself to withhold from her anything in the Hebrew Bible which the Septuagint did not represent," then we must assume that the Hebrew Bible itself had undergone a corresponding change and development, from the early phase in which it was known at about the third century B.C.E., which we possess in the Greek translation of the LXX, to the later phase current in the days of Origen. 2. Now the argument of unfairness to the Jew refers to religious disputations and implies that the discrepancies between the LXX and the Hebrew Bible are highly important from the theological point of view, with the LXX readings proving the case of the Christians. But we saw in paragraph III how unreliable the LXX is in this very respect. The case discussed there in subdivision A 2 shows that the Hebrew text with its reading לִבְנִי could well be taken as foretelling the coming of Jesus, in keeping with Matthew, while it is just the rendering of this verse as Septuagint's τα τεκνα αυτου which excludes such an interpretation. The same holds true of the examples listed there under numbers 4 and 5: The Hebrew Bible on Isa 42 1 and Zech 12 10 offers exactly the same text which Matthew used in Greek translation for his interpretation in a christological sense; but the respective LXX readings are decidedly useless for this purpose. Thus Swete's argument turns against him! 3. Swete has to admit that it "may be doubted whether Origen possessed the requisite knowledge of Hebrew." How, then, could he "indicate... the relation in which the old Alexandrian version stood to the current Hebrew text," in order "to restore the Septuagint to its original purity, i. e. to the Hebraica veritas?" For such an undertaking more than just an average knowledge of Hebrew is necessary! 4. What is the "Hebraica veritas"? This term is introduced here to explain the "original purity" of the LXX; in this case it is identical with the Hebrew Bible as current in or about the third century B.C.E., and thus materially different from the Hebrew Bible of the days of Origen, since he considers it unfair to fight the Jews with LXX quotations, which they do not possess in their Hebrew Bible (cf. above sub No. 1). But the context of this citation from Swete makes it clear that to him "Hebraic verity" and the Hebrew Bible text of Origen were identical. In other words: Origen aimed at the "restoration" of the LXX in such a way that it might be considered a Greek version of the Hebrew Bible of his own days, thus giving it a form which it had never had before. But a mere glance into the critical apparatus of Kittel's Biblia Hebraica with its numerous variant readings from the LXX is enough to convince us of the complete failure of his alleged attempt.

IX. A New Approach.

The main feature of the new evaluation of Origen's work here attempted consists in a complete break with the theories of the past, which are wholly based upon statements found in the works of early Christian writers. Though they lived so many centuries nearer to the time of Origen, they are not reliable as witnesses; for the several generations which separated them from Origen did their part in obscuring the plan and conception of the Hexapla in a mist of tradition. By following their lead, Swete became entangled in inner contradictions, as we have pointed out above.

We shall, therefore, go back to the original sources, and base our conclusions solely on the evidence of Hexaplaric statements themselves. We derive our material from Fridericus Field: *Origenis Hexaplorum quae supersunt* (2 vols., Oxford 1875). His collection has been carefully gone through and I hope that no essential item has been overlooked. What I offer here is not preconceived theories with a few examples to uphold them, and possibly at the same time unconsciously eliminating as immaterial other instances which might well be considered as proof against these theories. I wish to emphasize that while no attempt has been made to bring a complete list of the passages belonging to the various subdivisions — any such attempt would be futile, since from time to time new material comes to light, thus rendering today incomplete the complete list of yesterday — my collection presents no arbitrary selection. I have limited myself to the grouping and classifying of the material. The theories as to how to account for these phenomena thus emerge quite by themselves. In this fashion *we base our conclusions upon the internal evidence of Origen's work alone.*

X. The Septuagint according to the Hexapla.

The following paragraphs represent an attempt to arrange in a methodical way the material contained in Field's compilation, so as to allow us to arrive at conclusions regarding the nature of the sources which Origen utilized for the fifth column of his work. While listing the quotations here under the authority of Origen, it should be understood that it is Field to whom belongs the credit of having restored these readings, as well as the responsibility for the exactness of their wording and the correctness of the symbols under which they are brought.

§ 1. Septuagint quotations of the *Hexapla*.

The fifth column of the *Hexapla*, which was devoted to the LXX is being quoted under the following symbols: a. O' or οι O' b. al ex (=*alia exemplaria*). Both terms refer to Origen's LXX, but reflect two translations, which in their origin were entirely independent from one another. I already brought a few examples to prove this assertion of mine in *Festschrift P. Kahle* on pp. 45 f., and wish to add now just a few more: Dt 27 20: כנף: O': συγκαλυμμα; al ex: ασχημοσυνην. Dt 5 7: על פני: O': προ προσωπου μου; al ex: πλην εμου. Dt 19 14: ראשנים: O': οι πατερες σου; al ex: οι προτεροι σου. Nu 13 10: סודי: O': σουδι; al ex: σουρι. Ex 6 16 and Nu 3 17: גרשון: O': γεδσων; al ex: γηρσων. An interchange of Δ — P has no foundation in Greek palaeography, nor even in Greek phonetics, while a confusion of the corresponding letters ד — ר in the Hebrew alphabet is well attested (cf. *HPT* § 21).

Consequently, the readings quoted under O' and under al ex go back either to two independent translations of the entire Hebrew Bible, or to one genuine translation from the Hebrew and one revision of this Greek translation, which in turn must have been based upon a constant reference to the Hebrew Bible. Thus the interrelation between translation and revision would be comparable to the relation between Jerome's translation of the Hebrew Bible and the *Vetus Latina*. Whether these quotations represent two translations or only one translation and one revision thereof, in either case the Hebrew Bible text has to be presupposed as the basis for the revision and hence for the divergent readings *sub alia exemplaria*; they, therefore, reflect a new and independent translation at least of these Biblical passages.

On passages like Ps 104 18: לשפנים: O': τοις χοιρογρυλλιοις; al ex: τοις λαγωοις, as indicative of the respective country where such readings could originate, see my article in *Festschrift Kahle*, pp. 43 f.

We wish to emphasize that this differentiation between quotations from the fifth column of the *Hexapla* as O' and al ex has no basis in the sources from which they originate, but represent merely a *Notbehelf* of Field which enabled the editor to list both variant readings. While their sources quote them as genuine Hexaplaric LXX, we have just been able to prove that they reflect two independent translations. If this be the case, it is of interest to investigate whether Field's procedure in assigning the quotations to O' and al ex, respectively, is in keeping with the characteristics of these translations (cf. § 9). A few examples will illustrate what we mean: In § 5 I discussed (under a) the rendering of מתוך into Greek; but in Nu 26 62 Field lists the variants vice versa as בתוך בני: O': εν μεσω υιων al ex: εν τοις υιοις. In chapter XI b we proved that the asterisk-type offers a slavishly literal translation as against the free rendering into readable Greek by O'. This relation appears upset by the way in which Field arranges the readings in Ex 15 16: קנית: O': ον εκτησω; al ex: ελυτρωσω. Nu 6 19: את נזרו: O': την ευχην αυτου; al ex: την κεφαλην αυτου. Field is similarly inconsistent in Gen 46 8: הבאים: O': των εισελθοντων; al ex: των εισπορευομενων, compared with Dt 1 8: באו: O': εισπορευθεντες; al ex: εισελθοντες. Consequently we had to be careful in making use of Field's collection. Cf. also § 2.

§ 2. HEXAPLARIC SYMBOLS.

LXX quotations in the *Hexapla*, both O' and al ex, are often marked with an asterisk or an obelus, the exact form of which differs slightly in the various source-manuscripts. Practical consideration induces us to use ※ to indicate the asterisk, and ÷ for the obelus throughout this monograph. An ⌐ indicates the end of the quotation *sub asterisco* or *sub obelo*, respectively. Both asterisk and obelus may include a. the quotation in full, or b. merely a part of it; cf., e. g., a. Ex 12 41: ויהי בעצם היום הזה: O': ※ και εγενετο εν τη ημερα ταυτη ⌐. Gen 46 21: וארד: O': ÷ γηρα δε εγεννησε τον αραδ ⌐. b. Nu 22 23: ויך בלעם: O': και επαταξε ※ Βαλααμ ⌐. ib. 21 5: הקלקל: O': τω διακενω ÷ τουτω ⌐. A combination of both symbols in one and the same sentence may occur, too: see e. g. Nu 10 34: וינסו משנאיך מפניך: O': φυγετωσαν ÷ παντες ⌐ οι μισουντες σε ※ απο προσωπου σου ⌐. Ex 14 26: על מצרים: O': ÷ και επικαλυψατω ⌐ ※ επι ⌐ τους αιγυπτιους. Nu 10 31: ידעת חנתנו: O': ησθα ※ εν τη παρεμβολη ⌐ ÷ μεθ ημων ⌐.

Since the word or words encircled by asterisk or obelus are part of the full sentence, they must grammatically fit into their context; e. g. Ex 9 24: בכל ארץ מצרים: O': εν αιγυπτω; al ex: εν ※ παση τη γη ⌐ αιγυπτου. It is obvious that the words πάση τη γη are an addition to the O' reading εν αιγυπτω; but since the sentence thus newly formed is an entity in itself, its Greek language had to be made presentable. Consequently, the original dative αιγυπτω had to be changed into the genitive αιγυπτου. This observation can be varified on numerous passages. Note, e. g., the citation from Ex 14 26 in this paragraph: we may read και επικαλυψατω τους αιγυπτιους, thus excluding the word επι under asterisk, or even και επικαλυψατω επι τους αιγυπτιους, the full sentence. We realize that in either way the Greek syntax is quite correctly formed, for the compound επικαλυπτω is followed by the object in the accusative, or by a repetition of the particle of composition. This observation will furnish us with a criterion to establish the nature of Origen's critical work.

Those passages, where a Hexaplaric symbol is attested only by the *Syro-Hexaplaris* and not by a genuinely Greek text, are quoted in Field under *Aliter*.

In basing our investigation on these Hexaplaric symbols upon their occurrence in Field's collection of material, the question may be raised as to whether the particular symbol by which he marks a quotation is always reliably attested. A few examples will suffice to demonstrate the seriousness of this problem:

a. The asteriscus. בנות meaning daughter cities appears three times in Josh 17 11 *sub asterisco*, but in two different translations, according to the two citations: ויבלעם ובנותיה: O': Vacat. ※ και ιεβλααμ και θυγατερες αυτης ✕. ישבי עין דר ובנותיה וישבי תענך ובנותיה: O': Vacat. ※ και τους κατοικουντας ενδωρ και τας κωμας αυτης και τους κατοικουντας θααναχ και τας κωμας αυτης ✕.

חצר meaning village of the same district: Josh 19 22: ערים שש עשרה וחצריהן: O': Vacat. ※ πολεις εκκαιδεκα και αι κωμαι αυτων ✕. Ib. verse 30: ערים עשרים ושתים וחצריהן: O': ※ πολεις εικοσι δυο και αι κωμαι αυτων ✕. But ib. verse 38: ערים תשע עשרה וחצריהן: O': ※ πολεις δεκαεννεα και αι επαυλεις αυτων ✕.

משפחה: Josh 19 17: לבני יששכר למשפחותם: O': Vacat. ※ τοις υιοις ισσαχαρ κατα συγγενειας αυτων ✕. But ib.

verse 32: לבני נפתלי למשפחתם: O': Vacat. ※ τοις υιοις νεφθαλει κατα δημους αυτων ˣ. Cf. Nu 3 15: למשפחתם: O': κατα δημους αυτων; al ex: κατα δημους αυτων ÷ κατα συγγενειας αυτων ˣ. Thus, a doublet combines both translations, but assigns συγγενειας to the obelus-text.

This inconsistency in the rendering of Hebrew words into Greek may be taken as an indication that the different sources from which these quotations emanate reflect different recensions of the asterisk text on the passages in question; cf. also Gen 47 5: ויאמר: O': ※ και ειπε ˣ; al ex: ※ ειπε δε ˣ, with *JBL*, 1935, 90, paragraph XIV 2.

b. The obelus. Anticipating the results reached in chapter XI that readings marked by an obelus do *not* correspond to MT, we note cases like Dt 9 26: בגדלך: O': εν τη ισχυι σου ÷ τη μεγαλη ˣ (=בכחך הגדול). Ib. 21 9: הישר: O': το καλον ÷ και το αρεστον ˣ (=הטוב והישר). Here, strangely enough, it is exactly the word found in MT which is marked by the obelus.

In the course of the present monograph we refrained from making any use of such doubtfully marked quotations. Cf. also in chapter XI b the list of asteriscized passages without an equivalent in the MT.

§ 3. ASTERISK AND OBELUS READINGS ORIGINATE IN MARGINAL NOTES.

In those Hexapla-quotations where the otherwise smooth reading of the context is interrupted by an insertion marked by an asterisk or obelus, the explanation of such a breaking off of the sentence can best be found in an assumption that these insertions were originally meant as marginal notes, which afterwards were erroneously incorporated into the text without their first undergoing the necessary grammatical adjustment, as I pointed out in the preceding paragraph by referring to Ex 9 24. On the relation of readings *sub asterisco* and *sub obelo* to the Hebrew text which caused these marginal notes, cf. chapter XI.

a. *Asterisk readings.*

1. In several instances, the combination of asterisk insertion together with the Hexaplaric quotation sub O′ results in a translation of the full Hebrew Bible text, each one of these two sources representing a rendition of part of it, which in itself yields quite a good sense. These components now appear to have been put together merely mechanically, since they are not adjusted to the syntax of their context so as to form a unity from the grammatical point of view:

Nu 1 53: על עדת בני ישראל: O′: ※ επι την συναγωγην ✕ εν υιοις ισραηλ. (We should expect: ※ επι την συναγωγην ✕ των υιων ισραηλ.) The underlying Hebrew originals may be explained as על עדת ישראל and על בני ישראל (cf. *HPT*, § 123 a, c). Note the variation in the use of the particle επι and εν; cf. also the following example.

Josh 12 2: על שפת נחל ארנון: O′: ※ επι του χειλους ✕ εν τη φαραγγι ※ αρνων ✕. On the use of επι and εν see the preceding example. The corresponding Hebrew components are: על שפת ארנון and על נחל ארנון. A correct rendering of these two parts into one sentence would have resulted in: ※ επι του χειλους ✕ της φαραγγος ※ αρνων ✕.

Nu 17 6: כל עדת בני ישראל: O′: ※ πασα η συναγωγη ✕ οι υιοι ισραηλ. The Hebrew components are: כל עדת ישראל and בני ישראל. An adjustment of this asterisk-note to the context would lead to: ※ πασα η συναγωγη ✕ των υιων ισραηλ.

2. In other cases the quotation is being interrupted by an insertion, which is a literal translation of the hitherto only freely translated basic Hebrew word. But the inclusion of this insertion should have resulted in a corresponding change of the case of the following noun, an oversight which stamps the insertion as an intrusion from a note on the margin of the page:

Ex 21 8: אם רעה בעיני אדניה: O′: εαν μη ευαρεστηση ※ εν οφθαλμοις ✕ τω κυριω αυτης. Before εν οφθαλμοις crept into the text, the sentence was well formed: ευαρεστεω τινι, hence the dative τω κυριω. But now οφθαλμοις is the nomen regens to τω κυριω; consequently it should have been changed into του κυριου. Similarly

Josh 4 10: בתוך הירדן: O': εν ※ μεσω ✗ τω ιορδανη; simply εν τω ιορδανη is quite correct; but with the asterisk insertion we must insist on εν ※ μεσω ✗ του ιορδανου.

Josh 12 4: וגבול עון מלך: O': και ※ ορια ✗ ωγ βασιλευς; should read: και ※ ορια ✗ ωγ βασιλεως.

The government of the possessive pronoun in Greek syntax is a problem, which can not be dealt with here; but a sentence like

Nu 33 2: מסעיהם למוצאיהם: O': σταθμοι ※ αυτων και ✗ της πορειας αυτων is not Greek: και can not connect a nominative with a genitive. The original sentence σταθμοι της πορειας αυτων, with subsequent insertion of the possessive pronoun αυτων, should have been rearranged to read: σταθμοι ※ αυτων και ✗ η πορεια αυτων. Similarly

Josh 8 2: רק שללה ובהמתה תבזו לכם: O': και την προνομην των κτηνων προνομευσεις σεαυτω; this translation, too, according to another source, has been expanded by the inclusion of the possessive pronoun into: O': και την προνομην ※ αυτης και ✗ των κτηνων ※ αυτης ✗ προνομευσεις σεαυτω. A comparison between these two quotations reveals the thoughtlessness of the procedure; και cannot be used to connect an accusative with a genitive. A correction of the enlarged sentence into: και την προνομην ※ αυτης και ✗ τα κτηνη ※ αυτης ✗ προνομευσεις σεαυτω would have removed these difficulties.

3. Further evidence for the originally glossary nature of asterisk readings can be seen in

Nu 30 11: או אסרה אסר: O': η ο ορισμος; al ex: η ※ ον ωρισατο ✗ ορισμον; it is evident that the proper place for the relative sentence ον ωρισατο, being dependent on ορισμον, is only after this word, provided it were genuinely part of the full sentence. But being a later interpolation of a marginal gloss, it was wrongly placed; cf. later in § 7 our discussion of the various ways, how Dt 6 5 is quoted in the NT.

Nu 28 13: עלה: O': θυσιαν; al ex: ※ ολοκαυτωμα ⸓ θυσιαν. We are not concerned at present, whether θυσιαν is an equivalent for a Hebrew עלה or מנחה; but in al ex the addition of the asteriscized word should have resulted in ※ ολοκαυτωμα ⸓ θυσιας; cf. the examples listed under 2. Anticipating the results of our investigation in § 5, we wish to call attention to a similar faulty arrangement of words as a result of the inclusion of a marginal note into the text, which is equally being cited under al ex: Nu 3 51: את כסף הפדים: O': τα λυτρα (=את הפדים); al ex: το αργυριον τα λυτρα. The glossary character of το αργυριον is evident from the incongruity of the case of the following τα λυτρα; we would expect: το αργυριον των λυτρων; cf. also § 5 towards the end.

Ex 20 18: וינעו ויעמדו מרחק: O': ※ και σαλευθεις ⸓ εστησαν μακροθεν; the plural in εστησαν necessitates the change of the singular form of the participle σαλευθεις into the same number, too: ※ και σαλευθεντες ⸓ εστησαν μακροθεν.

The syntactic congruity of verbs refers not only to their number, but also to their tense. Consequently Jer 33 9: אשר אנכי עשה: O': α εγω ※ ειμι ⸓ ποιησω is an inner contradiction: present and future tense combined! The addition of ειμι is the result of a certain tendency consistently to translate אנכי by εγω ειμι, regardless of the context; cf. § 5 d.

Judg 3 8: ארם נהרים: O': συριας ποταμων has been expanded in other sources to: O': συριας ※ μεσοποταμιας ⸓ ποταμων. It is obvious that μεσοποταμιας originally represented another way of rendering ארם נהרים into Greek; it was put just after συριας, probably on account of the fact that both nouns end in *as* (genitive).

b. *Obelus readings.*

Judg 1 36: הָאֱמֹרִי: O': του αμορραιου ÷ ο ιδουμαιος. ※ This combination is a Greek equivalent of MT and הָאֱדֹמִי. The connection between the genitive and the following nominative is not clear at all, unless we consider ο ιδουμαιος as a mere gloss. On הָאֱדֹמִי as a variant to הָאֱמֹרִי, cf. *HPT*, § 36 in conjunction with § 21.

Jer 15 1: אֶל הָעָם הַזֶּה: O': προς αυτους. This corresponds to a Hebrew text: אֲלֵהֶם. Other sources bring this verse as: O': προς ÷ αυτους ※ τον λαον τουτον. Here αυτους impresses me as being a variant to τον λαον τουτον, since no conjunctive particle connects them syntactically. But even if this were the case, the result would be a tautology, since αυτους and τον λαον τουτον refer to the very same persons.

§ 4. OBELUS AND O' QUOTATIONS.

In order to prove the theory that the readings marked by a so-called Hexaplaric symbol have their origin in marginal notes, from which they later erroneously came into the text itself, I adduced thirteen asteriscized passages, but only two instances with an obelus. This proportion represents more or less accurately the occurrences of these symbols in the material from Origen's *Hexapla* as collected and presented by Field. We are now confronted with the problem, how to explain this apparent anomaly: does Field's collection convey a true picture of the original Hexapla, or is it a mere accident that a comparatively large number of asteriscized readings found their way into the works of Church Fathers and were thus preserved, while obelus readings for some reason or other were neglected from the very beginning? We have no means to solve this problem with certainty; but still there is a great likelihood that even in the original *Hexapla* the number of such obelus readings might have been rather limited. We shall see later that these marginal notes were the result of a comparison of the basic LXX text of the *Hexapla*, which is indicated here by O', with other Greek codices thereof (cf. § 9 under no. 10). The codex or the codices, the variant readings of which were marked with an obelus, must have belonged to the same textual family as the basic LXX text itself; for, indeed, it often happens that in the tradition concerning *Hexapla* quotations it is uncertain whether to assign them to O' as such or to an obelus text. A few instances will make this point clear:

a. The obelus is indicated in the *Syro-Hexaplaris*.

1. The tradition is uncertain regarding the full quotation:

I Kg 8 64: ואת המנחה: O': και τας θυσιας; Aliter: O': ÷ και τας θυσιας ×.

I Kg 9 9: s. v. מארץ מצרים: O': (εξ αιγυπτου) εξ οικου δουλειας; Aliter: O': ÷ εξ οικου δουλειας ×.

I Kg 17 22: s. v. וישמע יהוה בקול אליהו: O': και εγενετο ουτως και ανεβοησε; Aliter: O': ÷ και εγενετο ουτως και ανεβοησεν ×.

2. Only part of the quotation is involved:

I Kg 12 16: לאהליך ישראל: O': αποτρεχε ισραηλ εις τα σκηνωματα σου; Aliter: O': ÷ αποτρεχε × εις τα σκηνωματα σου ισραηλ.

I Kg 18 39: יהוה הוא האלהים: O': αληθως κυριος ο θεος; Aliter: O': ÷ αληθως × κυριος ...

I Kg 5 32: העצים והאבנים: O': τους λιθους και ξυλα τρια ετη; Aliter: O': τα ξυλα και τους λιθους ÷ τρια ετη ×.

I Kg 18 43: ויבט: O': και επεβλεψε το παιδαριον; Aliter: O': και επεβλεψε ÷ το παιδαριον ×.

II Kg 2 18: ויאמר אליהם: O': και ειπεν ελισαιε; Aliter: O': και ειπεν ÷ ελισαιε ×.

b. The obelus can be found in genuine Greek texts.

Gen 50 18: וילכו: O': και ελθοντες προς αυτον; al ex: και ελθοντες ÷ προς αυτον ×.

Ex 2 6: בכה: O': κλαιον εν τη θιβει; al ex: κλαιον ÷ εν τη θιβει ×.

Ex 11 3: בעיני עבדי פרעה: O': και εναντιον φαραω και εναντιον των θεραποντων αυτου; al ex: ÷ και εναντιον φαραω × και εναντιον παντων των θεραποντων φαραω.

Nu 2 7: מטה: O': και οι παρεμβαλλοντες εχομενοι φυλης; al ex: ÷ και οι παρεμβαλλοντες εχομενοι ※ φυλη.

Dt 15 3: s. v. ואשר יהיה לך: O': παρ αυτω; al ex: ÷ παρ αυτω ※.

Jer 35 18: אשר צוה אתכם: O': ενετειλατο αυτοις ο πατηρ αυτων; al ex: ενετειλατο αυτοις ÷ ο πατηρ αυτων ※.

Jer 36 6: במגלה: O': εν τω χαρτιω τουτω; al ex: εν τω χαρτη ÷ τουτω ※.

Ezek 24 18: ותמת אשתי בערב: O': ον τροπον ενετειλατο μοι εσπερας; al ex: ÷ ον τροπον ενετειλατο μοι ※ και απεθανεν η γυνη μου εσπερας.

Ezek 27 19: s. v. ויון: O': και οινον; al ex: ÷ και οινον ※.

Thr 2 16: בלענו: O': κατεπιομεν αυτην; al ex: καταπιωμεν ÷ αυτην ※.

On the relation of the readings marked with an obelus to their Hebrew text, cf. chapter XI under a.

These examples demonstrate the close affinity between the basic LXX text of the *Hexapla* and the one quoted *sub obelo*. Henceforth, in speaking of the obelus group, we shall include the quotations under O'.

§ 5. ASTERISK AND *ALIA EXEMPLARIA* QUOTATIONS.

In a similar way we can show that readings cited either *sub asterisco* or under the heading *alia exemplaria* (excepting those, which are specifically marked with an obelus, as e. g. the quotations listed above in § 4 b) are derived from sources which belonged to one and the same family of Greek textual tradition. We shall demonstrate this relationship by referring to the way, in which certain Hebrew words appear in Greek translation in Hexaplaric quotations *sub asterisco* and *sub alia exemplaria*:

a. מתוך: Ex 3 2: מתוך הסנה: O': εκ ※ μεσου ※ του βατου. Bearing in mind our remarks in § 2, we see in this quotation an amplification of the pre-asterisk reading: εκ του βατου. Thus we get two translations: εκ του βατου for O', and εκ μεσου του βατου for the asterisk type. Compare with these results the way, in which the same Hebrew phrase is rendered in Ex 3 4: מתוך הסנה: O': εκ του βατου; al ex: εκ μεσου του βατου.

b. פן: Dt 6 15, 7 25: פן: O': μη ※ ποτε ⌄; a combination of μη for O', and μηποτε for the asterisk-type; cf. Dt 4 16: פן: O': μη; al ex: μηποτε.

c. הנה: Ex 16 10: והנה: O': και ※ ιδου ⌄; the readings: και (for O') and και ιδου (for the asteriscus) combined; cf. Ex 14 10: והנה: O': και; al ex: και ιδου.

d. אנכי: Jer 33 9: אנכי עשה: O': εγω ※ ειμι ⌄ ποιησω; the personal pronoun is thus translated: εγω (by O') and εγω ειμι (by ※), although the fact that אנכי is here followed by a verb in the future tense (ποιησω) should have excluded the insertion of the present ειμι. The same remarkable combination of ειμι with a finite verb in the future tense we can notice in Ruth 2 13: ואנכי לא אהיה: O': (και ιδου) εγω; al ex: (και) εγω ειμι εσομαι. On אנכי as εγω ειμι in this textual type, cf. also Gen 50 5: הנה אנכי מת: O': Vacat. al ex: ιδου εγω ειμι αποθνησκω.

In these instances, the asterisk translation of a Hebrew phrase corresponds to that given elsewhere under al ex; we may, therefore, assume that the sources of asterisk and *alia exemplaria* quotations were members of one and the same group of text-witnesses. In other words, readings listed under al ex are in reality asterisk readings, whose asterisk has been omitted for some reason or other during the long history of text-tradition. On the carelessness of the copyists cf. Jerome's statement quoted here in chapter X § 10; cf. also the instance from Nu 3 51, brought in § 3 a 3 in connection with Nu 28 13.

§ 6. ORIGEN'S SOURCES.

We started in § 1 with the statement that LXX quotations of the fifth column of the *Hexapla* are referred to either sub O' or sub "al ex." In § 2 we had to add that Origen himself introduced the so-called Hexaplaric symbols in order to indicate the various sources from which certain readings emanated; cf. § 3.

It now seems as if Origen based his work upon a collation of four sources, which we would name after the respective authority under which they are quoted: the O', al ex, asterisk, and obelus texts. But in view of the fact that O' and obelus form one group (cf. § 4), and al ex and asterisk another (cf. § 5), we arrive at the conclusion that Origen consulted for the purpose of his work representatives (note the plural) of *two Septuagint families*: the obelus group (indicated by O' and ÷), and the asterisk group (indicated by al ex and by ※).

§ 7. LATER CONFUSIONS RESULTING IN DOUBLETS.

In § 3 we saw how some asterisk and obelus readings do not fit syntactically into their context — due to the incongruity of the case, number, word order, or the like — and thus suggest a theory that they were originally noted down as a variant on the margin of the respective line, from which they were afterwards erroneously taken into the text itself. In the cases dealt with there, these "variants," as we may call them, represent a Greek rendering of a Hebrew word or phrase, which had otherwise remained without a corresponding translation in the basic Hexaplaric LXX text. This fact can best be explained by assuming that these words or phrases were not contained in the Hebrew original of the basic translation; cf. chapter XI. With our MT in mind, the variant, therefore, merely supplements the current Greek text.

But there are quite a number of cases where the variants constitute another way of rendering into Greek a Hebrew word or phrase, which already appears in the current Hexaplaric LXX text. The nature of these variants may differ; they are sometimes Greek synonyms, a free translation as compared with the literal one of the basic text, or vice versa, representing a different exegesis of the underlying Hebrew text, etc.

If, by a scribal error, a marginal note of this kind happened to be included in the text, the result is that now a certain Hebrew word or phrase appears therein in two translations; this is termed a doublet.

Before we proceed to classify the doublets and base further

conclusions on this phenomenon, it might be deemed advisable to produce an example from a related ancient source in order to show the working process of such copyist's mistakes. Dt 6 5: ואהבת את יהוה אלהיך בכל לבבך ובכל נפשך ובכל מאדך is of great theological significance for the NT; Matthew, Mark and Luke quote it; and it is worth while to examine the way in which this verse appears in their respective Gospels: Matt 22 37 reads: αγαπησεις κυριον τον θεον σου εν ολη τη καρδια σου και εν ολη τη ψυχη σου και εν ολη τη διανοια σου. According to the three items mentioned in the Hebrew text, we have three nouns in Greek, which we would number consecutively as: 1. καρδια, 2. ψυχη, 3. διανοια. But Mark and Luke offer four nouns instead, the arrangement of which is interesting, too. Mk 12 30: και αγαπησεις κυριον τον θεον σου εξ ολης της καρδιας σου και εξ ολης της ψυχης σου και εξ ολης της διανοιας σου και εξ ολης της ισχυος σου. We will not concern ourselves here with the difference in the use of the particle, which results in a difference of the case for the noun; cf. above in chapter III b the classification under XII. It is obvious that ισχυος represents another translation of מאדך and thus forms a doublet to διανοιας according to our definition as given above. The arrangement of the nouns as compared with Matthew, is here: 1, 2, 3, doublet. Let us now consult Luke 10 27: αγαπησεις κυριον τον θεον σου εξ ολης της καρδιας σου και εν ολη τη ψυχη σου και εν ολη τη ισχυι σου και εν ολη τη διανοια σου. The same four nouns as in Mark, but their order is: 1, 2, doublet, 3.

In other words: the doublet ισχυς — the case is merely a matter of adjustment, cf. § 2, and does not matter here —, originally a marginal gloss, was taken into the text by the copyists of Mark and Luke; but the mistake did not produce the same results in these two cases; for each one of the copyists placed the gloss differently. This consideration leads us to the conclusion that in the case of a doublet it would be utterly wrong to assume mechanically that the first reading is the genuine translation or citation, and the second a later addition and therefore the doublet, or vice versa. Only inner criteria will have to be applied in order to solve this question for each case separately; cf. also our note on Ex 12 5 in § 8, e, β, 1.

§ 8. CLASSIFICATION OF THE DOUBLETS.

Two vertical strokes like // separate the two components of a doublet.

a. *Doublets traceable to their sources*

α. Asyndetic connections.

Gen 44 28: עד הנה: O': $αχρι νυν$; al ex: $ετι$. The combination of both results in: *alia*: $ετι$ // $αχρι νυν$.

Dt 13 18: כאשר נשבע: O': $ον τροπον ωμοσε$; al ex: $ον τροπον ωμοσεν$ ÷ $κυριος$ ˣ; *alia*: $καθως ελαλησε κυριος$. These readings asyndetically put together appear in: *alia*: $καθως ελαλησε σοι$ // $ον τροπον ωμοσε κυριος$.

Judg 9 4: בעל ברית: O' $Βααλβεριθ$; al ex: $Βααλ διαθηκης$; *alia*: $Βααλβερειθ$ // $διαθηκης$.

Lev 13 2: או בהרת (ספחת): O': (($σημασιας$)) $τηλαυγης$; al ex: $η τηλαυγης$; *alia*: $η τηλαυγης$ // $η αυγασμα$. Unlike the case of II Kg 1 3 which is dealt with in subdivision β, the particle $η$ is here part of the variant, and not an addition in order to connect the two parts of the doublet. For the source of the reading $αυγασμα$ cf. verse 4: בהרת: O': $τηλαυγης$; al ex: $αυγασμα$.

β. Connected by καυ or η.

Dt 7 1: רבים (1°): O': $μεγαλα$; al ex: $πολλα$; *alia*: $μεγαλα$ // $και πολλα$.

Dt 7 1: רבים (2°): O': $πολλα$; al ex: $μεγαλα$; *alia*: $μεγαλα$ // $και πολλα$.

II Kg 1 3: אלהים: O': $θεον$; al ex $προφητην$; *alia*: $θεον$ // $η προφητην$.

Cf. *JBL* 1935, 83, paragraph IV, the instance from Zech 7 3 where Theodoret similarly connects with $η$ the two readings forming a doublet. See also later under d β our remark on Judg 5 29. The reading under al ex in Dt 15 21 proves that και and η were conjunctive particles.

γ. Adjustment of the case of the second noun.

I Kg 22 38: את הרכב: O': το αιμα (free translation); al ex: το αρμα (literal); alia: το αιμα // εκ του αρματος. Cf. also later under b β 1 the last two examples.

δ. The source traceable for one reading only.
1. *Under alia exemplaria the first translation is quoted.*

Ex 30 8: תמיד: O': ενδελεχισμου // διαπαντος; al ex: ενδελεχισμου.
Lev 16 31: שבת שבתון: O': σαββατα σαββατων // αναπαυσις αυτη; al ex: σαββατα σαββατων. Cf. Lev 23 3: שבת שבתון: O': σαββατα αναπαυσις.
Dt 31 6: עמך: O': μεθ υμων // εν υμιν; al ex: μεθ υμων. Cf. also Lev 25 45: עמכם: O': Vacat. al ex: μεθ υμων; alia: εν υμιν.
Jer 48 13: מבטחם: O': ελπιδος αυτων // πεποιθοτες επ αυτοις; al ex: ελπιδος αυτων.

A combination of MT and a variant hereof is represented in II Sam 1 19: על במותיך: O': υπερ των τεθνηκοτων // επι τα υψη σου; al ex: περι των τεθνηκοτων σου. The first translation equals עַל מָתֶיךָ; the second corresponds to MT; cf. also verse 25: על במותיך: O': επι τα υψη σου.

2. *Under alia exemplaria the second translation is quoted.*

Ex 28 3: חכמה: O': σοφιας // και αισθησεως; al ex: [αισθησεως.
Ruth 2 16: וגם של תשלו לה: O': και βασταζοντες βαστασατε αυτη // καιγε παραβαλλοντες παραβαλειτε αυτη; al ex: καιγε παραβαλλοντες παραβαλειτε αυτη.

3. *Both translations combined by asterisk.*

Ex 26 13: בעדף בארך יריעת: O': εκ του υπερεχοντος των δερρεων // εκ του μηκους των δερρεων; al ex: εκ του υπερεχοντος ※ του μηκους ⳽ των δερρεων. The first translation in O' corresponds to: בעדף יריעת, the second to: בארך יריעת. Under al ex the first translation is quoted, with an asterisk insertion from the second. Thus, the enlarged al ex quotation reflects MT; cf. also later XII § 3.

b. *Doublets in O'-quotations.*

α. Combination of transliteration and translation.

1. *Transliteration first.*

Judg 1 11: קרית ספר: O': καριαθσεφερ // πολις γραμματων.
I Sam 7 12: אבן העזר: O': αβενεζερ // λιθος του βοηθου. Cf. ib. sub al ex: αβενεζερ ο σημαινει λιθος του βοηθου.
I Sam 15 8: החרים: O': ιεριμ // απεκτεινεν. The spelling ιεριμ is probably a mistake for εριμ; cf. *TRL* § 52.
I Sam 23 14: במצדות: O': εν μασερεμ (sive μασερεθ) // .... εν τοις στενοις. The reading μασερεθ is more likely to be the correct one. On the confusion between ד — ρ (=ר), cf. *HPT*, § 21.
I Sam 23 19: במצדות: O': εν μεσσαρα // εν τοις στενοις. In the Hebrew original, upon which the transliterated form is based, the text probably read במצודה in the singular; cf. I Sam 24 23: על המצודה: O': εις την μεσσερα // στενην.

2. *Translation first.*

I Sam 7 4: ואת העשתרת: O': και τα αλση // ασταρωθ. Cf. verse 3 והעשתרות: O': και τα αλση; Αλλος: ασταρωθ.
I Sam 21 8: נעצר: O': συνεχομενος // νεεσσαραν.
Jer 34 5: והוי אדון: O': ουαι κυριε // και εως αδου. We have to assume that the genitive αδου was substituted for αδον, which in turn was taken to be a Greek word (originally αδων), under the influence of εως. For a similar case of a misunderstood transliteration treated as a Greek word, see later I Sam 15 33 in e α.

β. Combination of two translations.

1. *Asyndetic connection.*

Judg 13 2: ממשפחת: O': απο δημου // συγγενειας. Cf. ib. 18 2: ממשפחתם: O': δημων; al ex: συγγενειων; similarly ib. v. 11.
Judg 15 5: ועד קמה: O': και εως σταχυων // ορθων.
I Sam 9 21: שבטי: O': σκηπτρου // φυλης. Cf. ib. 10 19: לשבטיכם: O': (κατα τα) σκηπτρα; al ex: φυλας; cf. also ib. verse 20.

I Sam 20 35: למועד: O': καθως εταξατο // εις το μαρτυριον.
Is 5 1: בקרן: O': εν κερατι // εν τοπω.
Is 40 13: ואיש עצתו יודיענו: O': και τις αυτου συμβουλος εγενετο // ος συμβιβα αυτον. Cf. 1 Cor 2 16: τις γαρ εγνω νουν κυριου, ος συμβιβασει αυτον.
Jer 5 15: לשונו: O': της φωνης // της γλωσσης αυτου.
Jer 43 6: את הגברים: O': τους δυνατους // ανδρας. Cf. ib. 44 20: על הגברים: O': τοις δυνατοις.

The following doublets are based upon the formation of two Hebrew words out of the consonants of the single word as found in the text (cf. *HPT*, § 37):

Judg 5 8: שערים: O': πολεις // αρχοντων. A combination of ערים and שרים.
Is 24 14: מים: O': το υδωρ // της θαλασσης. This corresponds to מים and ים; cf. later e β 1, the example from I Kg 18 44. On the adjustment of the case of the second noun, cf. above a γ.

2. Connected by και.

Judg 1 23: ויתירו: O': και παρενεβαλον // και κατεσκεψαντο.
Is 14 2: והתנחלום: O': και κατακληρονομησουσι // και πληθυνθησονται.
Is 24 8: שאון: O': αυθαδεια // και πλουτος.
Jer 52 7: החמתים: O': του τειχους // και του προτειχισματος.

c. *The obelus-text.*

a. Combination of translation and transliteration.

Josh 5 6: במדבר: O': εν τη ερημω // ÷ τη μαβδαριτιδι ×.
Judg 20 13: בני בליעל: O': τους ασεβεις // .... ÷ τους υιους βελιαλ ×.
Instead of τους ασεβεις read υιους ασεβεις. The doublet is misplaced; cf. our note on Ex 12 5 sub e β 1.

It will be noted that in both instances it is the obelus reading, which offers the Hebrew word in transliteration; cf. below § 9, 5 b.

A variant Hebrew text is reflected in Judg 1 10: קרית ארבע: O': καριαθαρβοκ // ÷ σεφερ ×. We have here MT and קרית ספר.

β. Combination of two translations.

1. *The second translation is sub obelo.*

א. Asyndetic connection.

Ex 25 17: כפרת: O': ιλαστηριον // ÷ επιθεμα ⨯.
Nu 12 12: כמת: O': ωσει ισον θανατω // ÷ ωσει εκτρωμα ⨯.
Judg 1 17: ויחרימו אותה: O': και ανεθεματισαν αυτην // ÷ και εξωλοθρευσαν αυτην ⨯.
Judg 1 20: ויורש משם את שלשה בני הענק: O': και εκληρονομησεν εκειθεν τας τρεις πολεις των υιων ενακ // ÷ και εξηρεν εκειθεν τους τρεις υιους ενακ ⨯.
Judg 1 27: ואת בנותיה: O': ουδε τας θυγατερας αυτης // ÷ ουδε τα περιοικα αυτης ⨯.
Is 3 23: הרדידים: O': θεριστρα // ÷ ˝κατακλιτα ⨯.
Thr 5 10: נכמרו: O': επελιωθη // ÷ συνεσπασθησαν ⨯.

ב. Connected by και.

Josh 9 4: ויצטידו: O': επεσιτισαντο // ÷'και ητοιμασαντο ⨯. The first translation reflects a text ויצטידו; on the confusion between ד — ר cf. *HPT*, § 21.
Is 3 2: גבור: O': γιγαντα // ÷ και ισχυοντα ⨯.
Is 66 7: והמליטה: O': εξεφυγε // ÷ και ετεκεν. Literal and free translation; cf. above sub a γ, the example from 1 Kg 22 38.

2. *The first translation is sub obelo.*

א. Asyndetic connection.

Ex 15 4: שלשיו: O': ÷ αναβατας ⨯ // τριστατας.
Ex 25 25: זר: O': ÷ στρεπτον ⨯ // κυματιον. Cf. also ib. verse 24 sub al ex.
Ex 27 20: זך: O': ÷ ατρυγον ⨯ // καθαρον.
Judg 20 15: בחור: O': ÷ νεανισκοι ⨯ // εκλεκτοι.
Judg 21 19: ללבונה: O': ÷ του λιβανου ⨯ // της λεβωνα.
Thr 2 20: עללי טפחים אם יהרג: O': ÷ επιφυλλιδα εποιησε μαγειρος φονευθησονται ⨯ // νηπια θηλαζοντα μαστους αποκτενεις.

The following two instances have their origin in the two possibilities of pronouncing the consonants of the respective Hebrew word:

Nu 17 2: הלאה זרה: O': ÷ το αλλοτριον τουτο ⋇ // σπειρον εκει. Vocalized as זָרָה (and הלאה read as הָאֵלֶּה) and זְרֵה (MT).

I Kg 6 1: למלך: O': ÷ βασιλευοντος ⋇ // του βασιλεως. This means: לִמְלֹךְ (MT) and לְמֶלֶךְ. It is noteworthy that in the first example it is the second translation which vocalizes according to MT, while in the second case it is the first one, sub obelo. Similar cases reflecting uncertainty of the pronunciation are listed in chapter III a 1; cf. further: II Kg 14 10: לִבְּךָ הַכָּבֵד: O': καρδια σου. ενδοξασθητι (=MT); al ex: η καρδια σου η βαρεια // ενδοξασθητι (=הַכְבֵּד and MT); ib. 16 18: הַשַּׁבָּת: της καθεδρας (=הַשֶּׁבֶת); al ex: της καθεδρας // των σαββατων (=הַשַּׁבָּת and MT); I Chron 13 6: שָׁם: O': ονομα αυτου (=MT); al ex: ονομα αυτου // εκει (=MT and שָׁם).

ב. Connected by και.

Gen 20 4: צדיק: O': ÷ αγνοουν ⋇ // και δικαιον.
Ex 33 5: עדיך: O': ÷ τας στολας των δοξων υμων και ⋇ // τον κοσμον. Cf. verse 6, listed in chapter XII, § 9 b.
Dt 7 15: אשר ידעת: O': ÷ α εωρακας και ⋇ // οσα εγνως. Cf. chapter XII, § 9 a, the instance from Gen 2 9.
Is 51 23: מוניך: O': ÷ των αδικησαντων σε ⋇ // και των ταπεινωσαντων σε.
A textual variant is involved in Micah 5 3: ורעה: O': ÷ και οψεται ⋇ // και ποιμανει. Reflecting וראה and ורעה; on the phonetic confusion between א and ע cf. HPT, § 3.

γ. The doublet is quoted under al ex.

Nu 3 15: למשפחתם: O': κατα δημους αυτων; al ex: κατα δημους αυτων // ÷ κατα συγγενειας αυτων ⋇. Cf. above b β 1, the instance from Judg 13 2.
Ex 30 10: הכפרים: O': του καθαρισμου; al ex: ÷ του καθαρισμου ⋇ // του εξιλασμου.

Nu 2 3: מזרחה: O': κατα ανατολας; al ex: ⨪ κατα νοτον ⨪ // κατα ανατολας.

II Kg 1 9: שר חמשים: O': πεντηκονταρχον; al ex: ⨪ ηγουμενον ⨪ // πεντηκονταρχον.

Jer 49 3: ספדנה: O': και κοψασθε; al ex: ⨪ και επιληπτευσασθε ⨪ // και κοψασθε.

d. *The asterisk-text.*

The doublet is arranged asyndetically, throughout.

α. The first translation is *sub asterisco*.

Dt 15 8: די מחסרו: O': ※ ικανον ⨪ // οσον επιδεεται.
Lev 26 16: בהלה: O': ※ σπουδη ⨪ // την απορίαν.
Ex 22 12: עד הטרפה: O': ※ μαρτυρα ⨪ // επι την θυραν. The asteriscized reading is based upon the masoretic vocalization עֵד; the doublet presupposes a pronunciation עַד.
Ex 16 4: דבר יום: O': ※ ρημα ⨪ // το της ημερας. The word-order suggests an explanation that ρημα was originally a marginal note to το, so as to conform more closely with the Hebrew word דבר; cf. in § 3 a the instance from Nu 30 11.

β. The second translation is *sub asterisco*.

Lev 22 18: נדריהם: O': ομολογιαν // ※ ευχων ⨪ αυτων.
Judg 5 29: אף היא: O': και αυτη // ※ δε ⨪. Cf. also Gen 28 8: וירא: O': ιδων δε // και; this doublet is a combination of και ιδων (cf. the quotation under al ex: και ειδεν) and ιδων δε. Similarly Dt 15 21: כל מום: O': μωμον; al ex: η // και πας μωμος; cf. on this above under a β the instance from II Kg 1 3, and below under f the instance from Nu 15 6.
Judg 11 34: יחידה: O': μονογενης αυτω // ※ αγαπητη ⨪.
Is 14 9: לקראת בואך: O': συναντησας σοι // ※ ερχομενου σου ⨪.
Jer 27 6: נתתי לו לעבדו: O': εργαζεσθαι αυτω // ※ δεδωκα δουλευειν αυτω ⨪.
Ezek 21 24, 25: ברא דרך תשים: O': επ αρχης οδου διαταξεις // ※ και συ ετοιμασον και διαταξον οδον ⨪.

e. *Al ex quotations.*

α. Transliteration and translation.

Judg 8 11: לנבח : O': της ναβαι; al ex: της ναβαι // και εξεναντιας The translation corresponds to a Hebrew word לנכח; on the confusion between ב — כ cf. *HPT*, § 23. The following ναβε in Field is merely a dittography of ναβαι, with a phonetic interchange between αι — ε. Similar cases of dittography are, e. g., Nu 6 3: יזיר : O': αγνισθησεται; al ex: αγνισθησεται ÷ απο οινου ⅹ (the words preceding it are: απο οινου και σικερα); Isa 14 8: ברושים : O': τα ξυλα ÷ του λιβανου ⅹ (from the following: η κεδρος του λιβανου).

Judg 8 33: בעל ברית : O': τω Βααλ διαθηκην; al ex: τον Βααλ-βερειθ // εις διαθηκην.

Judg 9 46: בית אל ברית : O': Βαιθηλβεριθ; al ex: οικου // Βηθηλ βερειθ. On the change from Βαιθ to Βηθ cf. *TRL* s. v. בית and חיל.

I Sam 15 32: מעדנת : O': τρεμων; al ex: εξ αναθωθ // τρεμων. The transliteration interprets the מ as an inseparable preposition, confuses ד with ת (cf. *HPT*, § 17) and changes its position by metathesis (cf. *HPT*, § 36); thus, a variant Hebrew reading מענתת results.

I Sam 15 33: וישסף : O': και εσφαξε; al ex: και εσφαξε // υιου σασειφ. υιου goes back to a misconception of ουιεσασειφ (cf. *TRL*, § 31 in conjunction with § 78 c) as two words, the first of which is a derivative of υιος; cf. a similar case of a transliteration being mistaken for a Greek word above b α 2, the instance from Jer 34 5.

β. Combination of two translations.

The arrangement is for the most part asyndetic. The source of one of these translations can be found in an O'-quotation.

1. *The O'-translation listed first.*

Ex 12 5: תמים : O': τελειον; al ex: τελειον // .... αμωμον. Between these two translations is αρσεν, the Greek equivalent of the following Hebrew word זכר. Thus, αμωμον is inserted in the wrong place; cf. similarly misplaced doublets below under 3 (the instance from Lev 4 25) and under f (the instances from Josh 6 5, Nu 15 6 and Isa 9 5), and above under c α (the instance from Judg 20 13); see also XII § 9 c.

Lev 1 3: לרצנו: O': δεκτον ※ αυτω ⨯; al ex: δεκτον αυτω // εξιλασασθαι.

Judg 16 16: למות: O': εως του αποθανειν; al ex: εως // εις θανατον.

II Sam 3 27: בשלי: O': ενεδρευων; al ex: ενεδρευων // εν παραλογισμω.

Judg 5 10: צחרות: O': μεσημβριας; al ex: μεσημβριας // και λαμπουσων.

In the following instances the two translations go back to differences in their basic Hebrew texts:

I Kg 18 44: מים: O': υδωρ; al ex: υδωρ // απο θαλασσης. Cf. above under b β 1 the instance from Is 24 14.

Is 2 5: O': και νυν; al ex: και νυν // συ. The underlying Hebrew text, though not to be found in MT, is ועתה — ואתה; on the confusion between א — ע, cf. *HPT*, § 3.

Thr 2 22: כלם: O': παντας; al ex: παντα // συνετελεσεν. O' pronounces the word as: כָּלָם, the doublet corresponds to MT; cf. in the following subdivision 2 the example from Isa 15 6.

2. *The O'-translation listed second.*

Dt 32 35: לעת חמוט: O': οταν σφαλη; al ex: εν καιρω // οταν σφαλη.

I Sam 1 16: לפני בת בליעל: O': εις θυγατερα λοιμην; al ex: εις προσωπον // εις θυγατερα λοιμην. With the results of § 5 in mind we note that the literal translation of פני and its derivatives is characteristic for the asterisk-group; cf., e. g., Gen 45 3: מפניו: O': Vacat. ※ απο προσωπου αυτου ⨯; Nu 10 35: מפניך: O': ※ απο προσωπου σου ⨯.

I Sam 16 14: ובעתתו: O': και επνιγεν αυτον; al ex: και συνειχεν αυτον // και επνιγεν αυτον.

Is 15 6: כלה: O': εκλειψει; al ex: πας // εκλειψει. Reflecting a pronunciation as כָּלָה and כָּלָה (MT), respectively; cf. above subdivision 1 the instance from Thr 2 22.

Thr 2 22: טפחתי: O': επεκρατησα; al ex: εξεθρεψα // και επεκρατησα.

3. Combination of O'-translation and asterisk-doublet.

Nu 15 11: בכבשים: O': εκ των προβατων; al ex: εκ των προβατων // ÷ εκ των αμνων ✕.

Lev 4 25: ונתן: O': και επιθησει; al ex: και επιθησει // .... ※ και δωσει ✕. The doublet is misplaced; cf. above subdivision 1, on Ex 12 5.

Is 1 27: ושביה: O': η αιχμαλωσια αυτης; al ex: η αιχμαλωσια αυτης // και ※ η αποστροφη αυτης ✕. The first translation pronounces the word וְשִׁבְיָה; sub asterisco the masoretic vocalization is presupposed.

Jer 46 20: יפה פיה: O': κεκαλλωπισμενη; al ex: κεκαλλωπισμενη // ※ καλλιστη ✕.

A variance in the basic Hebrew word is the underlying reason for

Jer 49 22: וידאה: O': οψεται; al ex: οψεται // ※ και επιπτησεται ✕. O' read וידאה; sub asterisco the masoretic word is translated. On the confusion between ר — ד cf. *HPT*, § 21.

f. Either translation is marked by an Hexaplaric symbol.

Dt 31 5: ככל המצוה אשר צויתי: O': καθοτι ενετειλαμην; al ex: ÷ καθοτι ✕ // ※ κατα πασαν την εντολην ην ✕ ενετειλαμην. Cf. also Josh 1 7: ככל התורה אשר: O': ※ κατα παντα τον νομον ✕ // καθοτι. In both instances, *sub asterisco* MT is translated, whilst the O' quotations reflect a reading כאשר (for כל המצוה אשר and ככל התורה אשר, respectively).

Josh 6 5: תחתיה: O': ÷ αυτοματα ✕ // .... ※ υποκατω αυτων✕. The doublet is misplaced; cf. above under e β 1 the instance from Ex 12 5.

Is 9 5: פלא יועץ: O': μεγαλης βουλης ÷ αγγελος ※ // ※ θαυμαστος συμβουλος ※.

Nu 15 6: או לאיל: O': ÷ και τω κριω....※ // ※ η τω κριω ※.
On the difference between και and η cf. our note on Judg 5 29 above d β. The doublet is misplaced, cf. here on Josh 6 5.

A difference in the underlying Hebrew texts may be the reason for

Josh 10 11: וימתו: O': ※ και απεθανον ※ // ÷ και εγενοντο ※.
A doublet within the asterisk-quotation occurs in

Is 9 5: אבי עד: O': ※ εξουσιαστης // ... πατηρ του μελλοντος αιωνος ※. On the dots indicating that the doublet is wrongly placed, cf. above on Josh 6 5.

g. *Doublets in both O' and al ex quotations.*

As a rule, one quotation offers the two doublets of the respective Hebrew phrase in full, while in the other quotation an effort towards stylistic adjustment into one Greek sentence is made.

a. The doublet reflects two different Hebrew originals.

Judg 1 14: ותצנח מעל החמור: O': και εγογγυζεν // και εκραζεν απο του υποζυγιον; al ex: και εγογγυζεν επανω του υποζυγιον // και εκραζεν απο του υποζυγιου. The variant in the translation of the particle as επανω and απο reflects corresponding readings על and מעל in the respective Hebrew original.

I Sam 14 47: לכד המלוכה: O': ελαχε του βασιλευειν // κατακληρουται εργον; al ex: κατακληρουται το εργον // του βασιλευειν. The difference in the rendering of the Hebrew noun as βασιλευειν and εργον probably corresponds to the pronunciation of המלכה (in defective spelling) as המלוכה or המלאכה; cf. *HPT*, § 38 a (the instance from I Sam 11 1 — I Chron 20 1) and § 40 c.

II Sam 19 8: ורעה לך זאת: O': και επιγνωθι σεαυτω // και κακον σοι τουτο; al ex: και επιγνωθι τουτο σεαυτω // οτι χειρον σοι εσται τουτο. The reading επιγνωθι reflects a Hebrew word ודעה; κακον equals MT. On the confusion between ר — ד, cf. *HPT*, § 21.

β. One translation is quoted
sub obelo.

Gen 15 11: על הפגרים: O': επι τα σωματα // ÷ επι τα διχοτομηματα αυτων ✕; al ex: επι τα σωματα // τα διχοτομηθεντα.
Ex 25 24: זר זהב: O': στρεπτα // κυματια χρυσα; al ex: ÷ στρεπτον ✕ // κυματιον χρυσουν.
Nu 15 19: תרימו תרומה ליהוה: O': αφελειτε αφαιρεμα // αφορισμα κυριω; al ex: αφελειτε αφαιρεμα τω κυριω // ÷ αφορισμα ✕.
Jer. 51 34: הממני: O': εμερισατο με // κατελαβε με; al ex: ÷ κατελαβε με ✕ // εμερισατο με.
Thr 1 12: הוגה: O': φθεγξαμενος εν εμοι // εταπεινωσε με; al ex: εταπεινωσε ÷ με ✕ // φθεγξαμενος ÷ εν εμοι ✕.

§ 9. RESULTS OF THIS CLASSIFICATION.

We now sum up the results of our classification of the doublets found in the Hexaplaric LXX quotations and state:

1. Doublets occur in O'-quotations as well as in those cited under the authority of *alia exemplaria*; (cf. § 8 b and e).

2. They consist of a combination of either
   a. a translation and a transliteration, or of
   b. two translations of the Hebrew original.

3. The two translations thus combined represent either
   a. an inner Greek differentiation of vocabulary and style; or
   b. a different interpretation of the same Hebrew text; or
   c. go back to two distinctly different Hebrew originals.

4. The difference between the two parts of a doublet, be they translation or transliteration, may also originate in an erroneous

conception of the one Hebrew text common to both of them, such as

  a. errors of pronunciation; they might serve as additional proof for the already established fact (cf. *TRL*, paragraph XV) that in Origen's day and even later no uniform and authoritative pronunciation of Hebrew can have existed, nor consideration for etymology (ib., paragraph XVI) and context (ib., paragraph XIX);
  b. confusion of letters on account of their resemblance
     α. in script (cf. *HPT*, §§ 20–32)
     β. in phonetic value (cf. *HPT*, §§ 1–19);
  c. dividing one Hebrew word into two, which leads to the assumption that in the basic Hebrew text no extra space nor any other indicator was used to separate the words from one another (cf. *HPT*, § 37).

5. A so called Hexaplaric symbol may differentiate one reading of the doublet from the other; if this be the case,
  a. the translation corresponding closer to MT has an asterisk; while
  b. the transliteration is marked by an obelus.

Since according to § 4, obelus and O' quotations belong to one family, as differentiated from the asterisk-al ex-group (§ 5), we wish to call attention to the following passages, where under O' a transliteration, and under al ex a translation is quoted: Gen 18 1: ממרא: O': τη μαμβρη; al ex: τη υψηλη. Ex 18 1: מדין: O': μαδιαμ; al ex: κυριον. Dt 3 17: הפסגה: O': την φασγα; al ex: την φαραγγα.

6. The existence of doublets further substantiates our conclusion in § 6 that the Hexapla is based upon two main sources; the examples listed in § 8 g show that their number did not exceed two; for the doublets quoted under the authority of O' are practically identical with those brought as *alia exemplaria*. With our conclusions in § 6 in mind, we would call these sources
  a. the obelus group, and
  b. the asterisk group.

7. Both groups must be regarded as genuine "LXX," since they are quoted as such and were embodied in the fifth column of the Hexapla, which contained the LXX.

8. The differences in their Hebrew original which they reflect (cf. above 3 c and 4) prove that they represent two independent translations of the Hebrew Bible into Greek.

9. While reconstructing their underlying Hebrew texts we realize the futility of any attempt to compromise between them and to unite them on a common basis. On the contrary, we shall have to look for the *two Hebrew Bibles*, each of which shares with the corresponding Greek translations their respective characteristic features and particular readings (cf. chapter XI).

10. The very fact that doublets also represent a combination of Greek synonyms, or otherwise demonstrate the two possibilities of expressing the same Hebrew word or phrase in Greek, is conclusive evidence that Origen made use of Greek Bible texts only, and did not consult the Hebrew Bible of his day (which is the hitherto generally accepted theory, see chapter VII). A mere glance into a Hebrew Bible would have convinced him that the Hebrew word in question was already represented in the Greek translation, thus excluding the possibility of combining two readings of this type into a doublet. On the other hand, while comparing two *Greek* Bibles, one offering, e. g., in I Kg 6 1: τοῦ βασιλέως, the other βασιλεύοντος, he was right in noting one as a variant (cf. § 3) on the margin, wherefrom it was later included in the text proper. Had Origen known enough Hebrew to verify these readings in the *Hebrew* Bible, he would have noticed that both are based upon one and the same Hebrew word למלך. Thus, Origen's work on the LXX consisted merely in collating Greek manuscripts belonging to one or the other of the two groups of translations (obelus and asterisk group), which in themselves are representatives of different Hebrew Bible types (cf. under no. 9).

The problem before us now is: to search for Hebrew Bible texts, which might justly be considered to reflect the Hebrew prototypes of the aforesaid two Greek Bible types (cf. above under 9). These Greek types were translations; and it may be said of them, too, what I pointed out some time ago with regard to the importance of the Variants in the larger Cambridge LXX edition for the historic development of the Hebrew Bible: "Eine Uebersetzung ist die Wiedergabe eines *bestehenden* Textes; also muss der Text jeder Septuaginta-Handschrift zu irgend einer Zeit auch tatsachlich existiert haben und im Umlauf gewesen sein" (*Septuaginta-Probleme*, Stuttgart 1929, 79).

But first we wish to establish beyond doubt the correctness of our assertion that there are only two and not more Greek LXX translations we have to reckon with.

§ 10. INNER GREEK DEVELOPMENT OF HEXAPLARIC SEPTUAGINT-QUOTATIONS.

In Field's collection of LXX quotations from the Hexapla, which forms the basis of this study (cf. our statement in chapter IX), we sometimes come across passages which are recorded under the authorities of O', *alia exemplaria* and *alia*, respectively; this latter term *alia* is to my knowledge at least in one connection (Ex 23 18) mentioned even twice. This might be taken as an indication for a corresponding number of independent sources of the fifth column of the Hexapla, namely three or even four translations, as against the two we upheld. However, an examination of quotations of this kind reveals them to be nothing else but later inner Greek developments of the genuine LXX quotations, the number of which does not exceed two. For like every other ancient text, these genuine passages were subject to changes by the hands of subsequent copyists, which, if wittingly made, may have been meant to improve on their language and style, or else were simply the result of the copyists' lack of understanding. In this connection it will be of interest to hear even Jerome complain of such misdeeds by the copyists. In *Epist.*, LXXI, 5 (cited by Harnack, *Bible Reading in the Early Church*, 100, note 2) he writes: "Opuscula mea ad describendum hominibus tuis dedi et descripta vidi in chartaceis codicibus ac frequenter admonui, ut conferrent diligentius et emendarent. ego enim tanta volumina prae frequentia commeantium et peregrinorum turbis relegere non potui.... Unde si paragrammata repereris vel minus aliqua descripta sunt, quae sensum legentis impediant, non mihi debes imputare, sed tuis et imperitiae notariorum librariorumque incuriae, qui scribunt non quod inveniunt, sed quod intelligunt, et dum alienos errores emendare nituntur, ostendunt suos." Cf. also above § 2.

This account of the bad experience which Jerome had from having to rely on copyists will help us understand the genesis of certain readings of the Hexapla. We shall illustrate this by a few examples, which we re-arrange in such a way as to demonstrate it beyond doubt that the underlying cause is solely inner Greek corruption and that they are entirely independent of the Hebrew Bible text.

a. *Three Greek readings based upon one translation.*

Ex 6 22: סתרי: O': σεγρει al ex: σετρει; alia: σεθρει. Considering the fact that ת as a rule is transliterated by ϑ (cf. *TRL*, paragraph XXIII under ת), which letter could phonetically be confused with τ, thus finally leading to a graphic confusion between T and Γ (cf. Thompson, Facs., 3), the chronological arrangement of these readings is just the reverse: σεθρει — σετρει — σεγρει.

Ex 23 28: וגרשה: O': και εκβαλεις; al ex: και εκβαλει; alia: και εκβαλω. The O' reading yields no sense, since not Israel but the הצרעה will be used as an instrument for driving the enemy out of the country. For this very reason the reading of *alia* in the first person is a corruption, too. Thus, εκβαλει represents the only genuine Greek translation, εκβαλεις being a graphic error, and εκβαλω an erroneous adjustment to the first person in the preceding verb αποστελω.

Nu 16 3: ויקהלו: O': συνεστησαν; al ex: συνεπεστησαν; alia: επισυνεστησαν. Compound and decompound, the latter differing in the order of the particles used for its formation.

Dt 7 1: כי יביאך: O': εαν δε εισαγη; al ex: οταν εισαγαγη; alia: εν τω εισαγαγειν. The various possibilities of rendering such conditional sentences in Greek can also be seen from Ex 6 13: להוציא: al ex: ωστε εξαγαγειν; alia: ινα εξαγαγη.

Dt 28 27: ובעפלים: O': εις την εδραν; al ex: εις τας εδρας; alia: εν ταις εδραις. Cf. *Tarbiz*, VI, 16, paragraph 7.

In the same manner the four readings of Ex 23 18 referred to above can be reduced to two. I bring them first in the same order as they are listed in Field's opus:

Ex 23 18: וזבחי: O': θυμιαματος μου; al ex: θυσιασματος μου; alia: αγιασματος μου; alia: θυμιασματος μου. I would suggest the following order: θυμιαματος — θυμιασματος — θυσιασματος. It becomes evident that these are merely inner Greek changes, which are in no way influenced by the Hebrew text. The only real variant reading that remains is αγιασματος; no further developments of this reading are recorded by Field.

b. *Three readings representing two genuine variants.*

1. The O' quotation in two forms.

Lev 4 7: העלה: O': των ολοκαυτωματων; al ex: της καρπωσεως; alia: της ολοκαυτωσεως. ολοκαυτωματων and ολοκαυτωσεως are two shades of one and the same rendering; cf. similarly κατακαυμα and κατακαυσις in *JBL*, 1935, 86, paragraph VIII.

Lev. 9 4: בלולה: O': πεφυραμενην; al ex: αναπεφυραμενην; alia: αναπεποιημενην. This arrangement indicates that under al ex a compound verb is cited of the O' reading; cf. also *JBL*, 1935, 87 paragraph IX; *Tarbiz*, VI, 16, paragraph 8.

Dt 24 14: לא תעשק: O': ουκ απαδικησεις; al ex: ουκ αδικησεις; alia: ουκ αποστερησεις. On the relation of the verb αδικησεις to its compound απαδικησεις cf. our remark to the preceding example.

Dt 32 43: יקום: O': εκδικαται; al ex: εκδικειται; alia: εκζητειται Cf. *JBL*, 1935, 85, s. v. נקם. On εκδικαομαι and εκδικεομαι cf. Walter Bauer, *Griechisch-Deutsches Woerterbuch zu den Schriften des Neuen Testaments*, 1928, Zur Einfuehrung, p. XV.

2. The al ex quotation in two forms.

The difference consists in a change of the word-order (cf. *Tarbiz*, VI, 19, paragraph 10).

Dt 22 17: והנה הוא: O': νυν ουτος; al ex: νυν αυτος; *alia*: αυτος νυν.
Dt 23 10: מחנה: O': παρεμβαλειν; al ex: εις πολεμον παρεμβαλειν; *alia*: παρεμβαλειν εις πολεμον.
Dt 28 66: לך מנגד: O': απεναντι των οφθαλμων σου; al ex: σοι απεναντι; *alia*: απεναντι σου.

This material shows that while the LXX quotations of the al ex type as a whole are well preserved, those of the O' group were subject to errors and changes by the later copyists. The reason for the different fate of these quotations may be sought in the fact that the O' type gradually became the authoritative text, displacing the al ex type, and was therefore more frequently copied.

c. *Three translations?*

The only instances to my knowledge which might, but not necessarily need, be considered as reflecting three genuine translations, are:

Ex 4 10: איש דברים: O': ικανος ειμι; al ex: ευλογος ειμι; *alia*: ευλαλος ειμι.
Lev 22 15: ירימו: O': αφαιρουσι; al ex: αφοριουσι; *alia*: αναφερουσι.
Nu 34 29: לנחל: O': καταμερισαι; al ex: καταμετρησαι; *alia*: κατακληρονομησαι.
Dt 31 5: לפניכם: O': υμιν; al ex: ενωπιον υμων; *alia*: εις τας χειρας υμων.

I would not attribute too much importance to these four instances; they surely cannot upset the results of our investigation. I am inclined to explain these cases as a Church Fathers' confusion between the fifth column of the *Hexapla* (containing the LXX) and some other column (containing a later Greek Bible translation).

XI. The Hebrew Bible according to the Hexapla.

a. The Hebrew Original of the obelus-group.

In the course of my studies on Hebrew grammar (for the time being see *TRL* and *HPT*) I became more and more convinced that the Hebrew Pentateuch of the Samaritans does not represent the Bible of the heretic sect of the Samaritans, but was originally another recension of the Hebrew Pentateuch, which might well compare with our MT. Comparing this form of the Hebrew Pentateuch with the obelus readings of the Hexapla, I was surprised to see how many agreements between both of them could thus be established. In keeping with my policy throughout this monograph, I do not aim at completeness in the following list; all I have in mind is to demonstrate the close affinity of the Hebrew and Greek texts. To this end I quote first, as always here, the respective passage of the Hebrew Bible in its Masoretic form:

Gen 1 14: יהי מארת ברקיע השמים: O': γενηϑητωσαν φωστηρες εν τω στερεωματι του ουρανου ÷ εις φαυσιν επι της γης ×; cf. in the Samaritan Pentateuch: יהי מאורות ברקיע השמים להאיר על הארץ.

Gen 4 8: ויאמר קין אל הבל אחיו: O': και ειπε καιν προς αβελ τον αδελφον αυτου ÷ διελϑωμεν εις το πεδιον ×; cf. *SAM*: ויאמר קין אל הבל אחיו נלכה השדה.

Ex 4 6: ויוצאה: O': και εξηνεγκε αυτην ÷ εκ του κολπου αυτου ×; cf. *SAM*: ויוציאה מחיקו.

Ex 8 5: ומבתיך: O': ÷ και απο του λαου σου × και εκ των οικιων υμων; cf. *SAM*: ומבתיך ומעבדיך ומעמך.

Ex 12 40: במצרים: O': εν γη αιγυπτω ÷ και εν χανααν ×; cf. *SAM*: בארץ כנען ובארץ מצרים.

Ex 22 4: בשדה אחר: O': αγρον ετερον ÷ αποτισει εκ του αγρου αυτου κατα το γεννημα αυτου · εαν δε παντα τον αγρον καταβοσκηση ×; cf. *SAM*: בשדה אחר שלם ישלם משדהו כתבואתה ואם כל שדה יבעה.

Ex 26 16: ארך הקרש: O': ποιησεις τον στυλον τον ενα; al ex: ※ μηκος × ÷ ποιησεις × τον στυλον ÷ τον ενα ×; cf. *SAM*:

ארך הקרש ה א ח ד; on ÷ ποιησεις ⨯ cf. verses 10 and 20, where in *SAM* the verb תעשה is added.

Ex 33 2: את הכנעני האמרי והפרזי החוי והיבוסי: O': τον αμορραιον και τον χετταιον και φερεζαιον και γεργεσαιον και ευαιον και ιεβουσαιον και χαναναιον; al ex: τον χαναναιον ÷ και ⨯ τον αμορραιον και τον χετταιον και τον φερεζαιον ÷ και τον γεργεσαιον ⨯ και τον ευαιον και τον ιεβουσαιον; cf. *SAM*: את הכנעני ו ה א מ ר י והחתי ו ה ג ר ג ש י והפרזי והחוי והיבוסי. Similarly in Ex 34 11: al ex: ÷ και τον γεργεσαιον ⨯ has its equivalent in the addition of *SAM*: ו ה ג ר ג ש י.

Ex 35 22: וכומז: O': ÷ και εμπλοκια ⨯ και περιδεξια; cf. *SAM*: ע נ י ל וכומז.

Lev 19 20: בקרת תהיה: O': επισκοπη εσται ÷ αυτοις ⨯; similarly *SAM*: בקרת תהיה לו.

Nu 1 44: איש אחד לבית אבתיו היו: Aliter: O': ανηρ εις ÷ κατα φυλην μιαν, κατα φυλην ⨯ εις οικον πατριας αυτων ησαν; cf. *SAM*: איש אחד ל מ ט ה א ח ד ל מ ט ה בית אבתם היו.

Dt 9 28: פן יאמרו הארץ: O': μη ειπωσιν ÷ οι κατοικουντες την γην ⨯; similarly *SAM*: פן יאמרו ע ם הארץ.

Dt 10 11: לפני העם: O': εναντιον του λαου ÷ τουτου ⨯; cf. *SAM*: לפני העם ה ז ה.

Dt 14 8: ולא גרה: O': και ÷ ονυχιζει ονυχιστηρας οπλης και τουτο μηρυκισμον ⨯ ου μαρυκαται; cf. *SAM*: ו ש ס ע ש ס ע פ ר ס ה והוא גרה לא יגור.

Dt 18 5: לעמד לשרת בשם יהוה: O': παρεσταναι ÷ εναντι κυριου του θεου ⨯ λειτουργειν ÷ και ευλογειν ⨯ επι τω ονοματι αυτου; cf. *SAM*: לעמד ל פ נ י יהוה א ל ה י ך לשרתו ו ל ב ר ך בשמו.

The preceding examples show the direct interdependence between the obelus type and the corresponding textual readings of the Hebrew Pentateuch of the Samaritans. But the relationship between these two Bible texts can also be demonstrated indirectly by certain characteristics in the structure of the narrative (*Formgeschichte*), which they have in common: In Gen 31 11 ff. Jacob tells Rachel and Lea of a vision which he had in connection with and approving of his intended return to his native land: ויאמר אלי מלאך האלהים בחלום יעקב ואמר הנני: ויאמר שא נא עיניך וראה כל העתדים העלים על הצאן עקדים נקדים וברדים כי ראיתי

את כל אשר לבן עשה לך: אנכי האל בית אל אשר משחת שם מצבה אשר נדרת
לי שם נדר עתה קום צא מן הארץ הזאת ושוב אל ארץ מולדתך. But we
search the Bible in vain for the original narrative of this vision
and the time and the place when and where it happened in
order to confirm Jacob's report. The MT is here of no use; but
the Samaritan Pentateuch brings after Gen 30 36 such a report,
in the same words as used in both MT and Sam later on in
Gen 31 11–13, merely changing the first person of ואמר into the
third ויאמר so as to fit in the context as the annalists record.

Similarly in Gen 44 22: Judah argues with Joseph for the
release of Benjamin and says: ונאמר אל אדני לא יוכל הנער לעזב את
אביו ועזב את אביו ומת. In MT, no record of the original remark
of the brothers to this effect is preserved. But here, too, it is
the *SAM*, which on Gen 42 16 offers this report, again in the
same words as *SAM* and MT have it on Gen 44 22, with the first
person ונאמר changed into the third ויאמרו. Thus, the reader of
the Pentateuch in the Samaritan recension is in a position to
ascertain that the vision of Jacob and the argument of Judah
are not merely made up *ad hoc*, because Jacob and Judah needed
them in their respective situation, but are well founded on the
preceding records of the objective annalist. In other words:
the historic narrative is now complete: The vision of the angel
leads Jacob to action; the brothers premonition, that Benjamin's
departure from his father's house may cause the latter's death,
is about to become true.

This characteristic of the *SAM* has a parallel in the obelus
text: In Josh 6 26 Joshua curses the man, who might attempt
to rebuild the city of Jericho, which he had just destroyed.
However, his curse did not deter later generations; cf. I Kg 16 34;
but the curse became true. Origen on Josh 6 26 adds *sub obelo*
the report of I Kg 16 34.

According to Josh 16 10 the Canaanites remained as a tri-
butary nation in Gezer in the midst of the Ephraimites עד היום
הזה. Origen adds *sub obelo* the passage I Kg 9 16 where the final
destruction of Gezer by Pharaoh is reported; the time-limit
for "unto this day" is thus given. In these cases the historic
narrative of the book of Joshua appears now complete, as far
as Biblical sources are concerned.

As similar cases I wish to note: Nu 14 22, 23: כל האנשים הראים את כבדי ואת אתתי אשר עשיתי במצרים . . . . אם יראו את הארץ. Here the punishment is pronounced that none of the generation which was redeemed from Egypt shall see the promised land. But the verses 30 and 33 grant mercy to their children, who will be privileged to enter it. Origen limits right from the start the judgment of v. 23 to the adult generation by adding *sub obelo* Deut 1 39.

Josh 20 3: here Origen quotes *sub obelo* Nu 35 12. I am under the impression that these additions in the *SAM* and *sub obelo* in Origen reflect one and the same tendency in narrating Biblical history: to supplement the running narrative from related sources, so as to present the reader with a complete description of the events.

I do not intend to advocate a theory that the Samaritan Pentateuch as it presents itself to us now is *the* Hebrew original of the Greek translation from which citations marked by an obelus in the *Hexapla* emanated. I have already demonstrated that our Samaritan Pentateuch must not be identified with that textual form, under which it was known and published even as late as the days of Jerome; see my article "The Targum Onkelos in its Relation to the Masoretic Text" in *PAAJR*, VI (1935), 312 ff. All I mean to say in explaining this coincidence between the quotations *sub obelo* and the actual Hebrew readings of the Samaritan Pentateuch is that the Hebrew Bible, which served as original to that particular type of the LXX which we call the obelus type, belonged to a family of Hebrew Bible tradition, an offspring of which we still possess in the Samaritan Pentateuch.

One more point remains, which has to be clarified: The obelus group of LXX citations is still preserved representing nearly all the books of the OT, while the Samaritan Pentateuch embraces, as the name indicates, merely the Pentateuch. How, then, shall we account for the Hebrew original of the remaining parts of the OT? We shall realize the full importance of this problem if we recall to our minds that the obelus *group* of the Hexaplaric LXX text consists not only of those quotations which are marked by an obelus, but also includes the numerous citations listed under O' and spread over all the OT; cf. especially the results we arrived at concerning codex B in chapter XIV. Consequently, we shall have to assume that the Samaritan Hebrew Bible originally included the entire OT. This assumption falls in line with the results I arrived at in my grammatical studies. But at the present stage of my researches I consider it as premature to advance any theories on this point; I hope to be able to take up this problem in the near future, in connection with an evaluation of the material offered in *HPT*. For the time being I limit myself to the conclusion that the *obelus-group of the LXX according to the Hexapla was a translation into Greek of a Hebrew Bible, which at that time covered all of the OT and of which we still have in the Samaritan Pentateuch a direct offspring in Hebrew.*

b. The Hebrew Original of the Asterisk Group.

Generally speaking, the readings marked by an asterisk as well as those cited under al ex are exact translations into Greek of the respective Hebrew passages according to the Masoretic text. I wish to demonstrate the painstaking care which the asterisk type takes in order to give an exact and literal translation of the MT, by pointing out a few examples, where such slavishly literal translations *sub asterisco* spoil the otherwise readable Greek of the respective sentence, and result in tautology, since the asteriscized words are already contained in the free renderings under O':

Gen 32 14: מן הבא בידו : O': ων εφερεν ※ εν χειρι αυτου ⨯.

Gen 33 1: וישא יעקב עיניו : O': αναβλεψας δε ιακωβ ※ τοις οφθαλμοις αυτου ⨯.

Gen 34 21: רחבת ידים : O': πλατεια ※ εν χερσιν ⨯.

Ex 18 7: וישאלו איש לרעהו לשלום : O': και ησπασαντο αλληλους ※ εις ειρηνην ⨯.

Dt 1 7: ובחוף הים : O': και παραλιαν ※ θαλασσης ⨯.

Dt 2 5: עד מדרך כף רגל : O': ουδε βημα ※ ιχνους ⨯ ποδος.

Ps 104 25: ורחב ידים : O': και ευρυχωρος ※ χερσιν ⨯; cf. Judg 18 10.

But in view of the fact that some readings of this asterisk type can be found, which do not have their equivalent in MT, we would prefer to formulate our statement in a less positive way, and say: it is evident that the Hebrew Bible used as an original for that Greek translation quotations from which are brought in Field's collection of material *sub asterisco* or under al ex, was most closely related to that textual family of the Hebrew Bible which is known to us as MT.

It is superfluous to bring examples for the agreement between the asterisk group and MT; this is the rule, and the reader can convince himself by opening Field at mere chance. We, therefore, confine ourselves to prove the existence of exceptions: asterisk readings without a corresponding Hebrew original in our MT; for another possible explanation cf. chapter X § 2 on the reliability of the tradition concerning the Hexaplaric symbols.

Lev 22 21: ואיש כי יקריב: O': και ανθρωπος ος αν προσενεγκη ※ τα δωρα αυτου κατα πασαν ομολογιαν αυτων η κατα πασαν αιρεσιν αυτων ✕; cf. Lev 22 18.

Josh 9 24: ונעשה: O': και εποιησαμεν; al ex: ※ ως ουχ υπελειφθη εν ημιν πνευμα ✕ και εποιησαμεν; cf. Josh 2 11.

Josh 11 14: בני ישראל: O': οι υιοι ισραηλ ※ κατα το ρημα κυριου ο ενετειλατο τω ιησου ✕; cf. Josh 8 27.

Josh 22 16: כל עדת יהוה: O': πασα η συναγωγη κυριου ※ οι υιοι ισραηλ ✕; probably on account of verse 12: כל עדת בני ישראל.

Judg 4 9: ותאמר: O': και ειπε; Aliter: O': και ειπε ※ προς αυτον δεββωρα ✕; on the addition of the subject cf. my *Septuagintaprobleme*, 60 and *HPT*, § 117 c and § 122 a; further: Gen 29 12: ויגד יעקב: O': και απηγγειλεν ※ ιακωβ ✕.

Judg 4 9: קדשה: O': εκ καδης; Aliter: O': εις κεδες ※ της νεφθαλι✕; cf. verse 6.

Judg 9 54: אשה: O': γυνη; Aliter: O': ※ οτι ✕ γυνη; cf. the following passages, where οτι appears *sub asterisco*, corresponding to MT כי: Dt 15 8: כי פתח: O': ※ οτι ✕ ανοιγων; Ps 116 16: כי אני: O': ※ οτι ✕ εγω; Ps 118 10: כי: O': ※ οτι ✕.

I Sam 20 9: ויאמר יהונתן: O': και ειπεν ιωναθαν ※ προς δαυιδ ✕ cf. verses 4, 11 and 12.

I Kg 21 29: בימי: O': ※ αλλ ✕ εν ταις ημεραις.

II Kg 19 16: אֶת דִּבְרֵי: O': ※ παντας ✕ τους λογους; cf. in the following passages πας and its derivatives *sub asterisco*, while MT offers the equivalent form of כל: Dt 4 19; 5 23, 26, 28; 12 2, 21.

Amos 6 8: מתאב: O': ※ διοτι ✕ βδελυσσομαι; cf. similarly Zech 13 5: אִישׁ עֹבֵד אֲדָמָה אָנֹכִי: O': ※ διοτι ανθρωπος εργαζομενος την γην εγω ειμι ✕; thus, *sub asterisco* MT is translated with διοτι as introductory particle.

C. THE OLDEST MANUSCRIPTS OF THE BIBLE IN GREEK.

XII. CODICES B AND A ON THE PENTATEUCH.

In *TRL*, paragraph XXXII, I showed that "by applying the results of this study to the LXX, we are in a position to differentiate between the various sources, by the combination of which an apparently uniform LXX text arose" (*TRL*, 46). I thus made it clear that both codices, B and A, "not only when considered as entities covering the entire Bible, but even on the single Biblical books, go back to different sources .... We thus realize that one of the most significant criteria of the works of those early centuries is their mixed type" (ib.).

We now wish to substantiate this statement by an examination of the LXX on the Pentateuch, since this part of the LXX represents, according to Jerome's testimony, a more careful translation of the Hebrew text than the rest of it: "accedit ad hoc quod quoque Josephus, qui LXX interpretum proponit historiam, *quinque* tantum ab eis *libros Moysii translatos* refert, quos nos quoque *confitemur plus quam ceteros cum Hebraicis consonare.*" (*Hieronymi quaestiones hebraicae in libro Geneseos* a recognitione Pauli de Lagarde, Lipsia, 1886, 2 f.). We shall base our investigation on Swete's edition. In this edition for the first time the text is taken from Codex B, except for the missing chapters Gen 1–46 28, where Codex A is being substituted. This combination of the two oldest manuscripts of the LXX on the Pentateuch will be the basis for our examination, too, which will thus shed light upon both of them.

This method of basing the text of the LXX edition on codex B and merely filling the missing chapters according to codex A, has been followed also in subsequent editions: the larger Cambridge edition by Brooke-McLean, and Alfred Rahlfs in his *Septuaginta id est Vetus Testamentum Graece iuxta LXX interpretes*, (Stuttgart 1935). It may be of interest to note here that out of the approximately seventy doublets from the LXX on the Pentateuch alone which we are going to discuss here, only in the following five cases has one component of the doublet been eliminated by Rahlfs from his basic text: Gen 23 13; Ex 25 23; Lev 8 5; Dt 4 20 and 8 4. Rahlfs does not account for the principles, which have been guiding him in his selection: which one of the two parts of a doublet to retain and which to reject. But we wish to emphasize that we cannot agree with the results of his selections. In Lev 8 5, זה הדבר, he preserves τουτο εστιν το ρημα and eliminates τουτο εστι; but in § 9a we are going to prove that "the literal translation of דבר by ρημα is characteristic for the asterisk type of the Hexaplaric LXX"; and since codex B as an entity "shows close affinity to the obelus type" (below ch. XV towards the end), Rahlfs has thus given the preference exactly to the wrong component. In Lev 15 1 he simply changes the position of και ααρων; he thus obtains, it is true, a smoothly worded verse, but a verse of his own making (cf. § 1). And the remaining more than sixty doublets he left unchallenged at all. This shows, how far his publication is from a real edition of the LXX!

Our own procedure will be similar to that which we applied in discussing the *Hexapla*; here, too, the existence of doublets proves to be most helpful. By our very method of grouping and classifying them we shall indicate their origin and finally arrive at conclusions as to the nature and the main characteristics of the two genuine texts in the combination of whose readings our doublets originate. The readings of the basic LXX text (B or A, respectively) of Swete's edition will be quoted here under G.

In order to save space, I refrained as far as feasible from bringing evidence for the separate use of each of these components of the doublets as equivalents of the respective Hebrew words. Such passages can easily be traced with the help of Hatch and Redpath's *Concordance*.

§ 1. THE DOUBLET ORIGINATES IN A MARGINAL NOTE.

This is obvious from the fact that doublets were inserted at a wrong place, where they do not fit into the syntax of the sentence:

Gen 24 5: אחרי: G: μετ εμου // οπισω. οπισω was noted as a variant to μετα; cf. *JBL*, 1935, 84, paragraph VI s. v. עם. The two translations in full would be: μετ εμου // οπισω μου; cf. Gen 24 39: אחרי: G: μετ εμου.

Ex 28 32: בתוכו: G: εξ αυτου // μεσον. In readable Greek, the inclusion of μεσον, which in itself is an exact rendering of תוך according to the asterisk type of the Hexaplaric LXX (cf. X, § 3 a, the instance from Josh 4 10) would result in εκ μεσου αυτου.

Lev 15 1: אל משה ואל אהרן לאמר: G: προs μωυσην λεγων // και ααρων. The correct word-order would be: προs μωυσην και ααρων λεγων. Prior to the inclusion of this gloss, the Greek text contained no reference to Aaron.

§ 2. THE SOURCES OF THE DOUBLET.

a. *The obelus text forms one source.*

Gen 20 4: צדיק: G: αγνοουν // και δικαιον; cf. O': ÷ αγνοουν ✕ και δικαιον.

Ex 15 4: שלשיו: G: αναβαταs // τριστατας; cf. O': ÷ αναβαταs ✕ τριστατας; cf. also Ex 14 7: ושלשם: G: και τριστατας; on the other hand, αναβατης is the equivalent of Hebrew פרש.

Ex 33 5: עדיך: G: τας στολας των δοξων υμων // και τον κοσμον; cf. O': ÷ τας στολας των δοξων υμων και ✕ τον κοσμον.

Ex 25 17: כפרת: G: ιλαστηριον // επιθεμα; cf. O': ιλαστηριον ÷ επιθεμα ✕.

Nu 15 19: תרומה: G: αφαιρεμα // αφορισμα; cf. al ex: αφαιρεμα τω κυριω ÷ αφορισμαι ×. תרומה is translated by G in Nu 15 20: αφαιρεμα, in Ex 29 28: αφορισμα.

b. O' and al ex texts combined.

Ex 34 15: ליושב: G: τοις ενκαθημενοις // προς αλλοφυλους; cf. O': τοις εγκαθημενοις; al ex: προς αλλοφυλους.

c. Stylistic adjustment of O' and al ex readings.

Gen 15 11: הפגרים: G: τα σωματα // τα διχοτομηματα; cf. O': επι τα σωματα ÷ επι τα διχοτομηματα αυτων ×; al ex: επι τα σωματα τα διχοτομηθεντα. Cf. also Lev 1 8: הנתחים: G: τα διχοτομηματα.

§ 3. THE DOUBLET PRESERVES THE FULL SOURCE OF AN ABRIDGED ASTERISK-READING.

Ex 26 13: בעדף בארך יריעת: G: εκ του υπερεχοντος των δερρεων // εκ του μηκους των δερρεων; cf. al ex: εκ του υπερεχοντος ※ του μηκους × των δερρεων; see also above X § 8 a δ 3.

§ 4. COMBINATION OF LITERAL AND FREE TRANSLATIONS.

Gen 3 6: לעינים: G: τοις οφθαλμοις // ιδειν.
Gen 3 14: גחנך: G: τω στηθει σου // και τη κοιλια; cf. Lev 11 42: על גחון: G: επι κοιλιας; Ex 28 30: על לב אהרן: G: επι του στηθους ααρων, also a free translation.
Gen 23 13: באזני: G: εις τα ωτα // εναντιον; cf. ib. verse 16: באזני: G: εις τα ωτα; Gen 44 18: באזני: εναντιον.
Nu 6 7: על ראשו: G: επ αυτω // επι κεφαλης αυτου.

§ 5. DIFFERENCE IN THE EXEGESIS.

Gen 18 10: כעת: G: κατα τον καιρον τουτον // εις ωρας; cf. ib. 21 22; 38 1: בעת ההיא: G: εν τω καιρω εκεινω; Ex 9 18: כעת: G: ταυτην την ωραν.

Ex 27 20: למאור: G: εις φως // καυσαι.
Lev 26 22: השדה: G: τα αγρια // της γης; an adjective in the nominative and a noun in the genitive; cf. similarly Ex 1 19: המצרית: O': αιγυπτου; al ex: αιγυπτιαι; Ps 104 4: אש להט: G: πυρ φλεγον, quoted in Heb 1 7 as πυρος φλογα (the context requires the accus.).
Nu 27 14: להקדישני: G: αγιασαι με // ουχ ηγιασατε με. On the interpretation of the particle ל as negation (=לא), cf. Gen 4 15; 30 15: לכן: G: ουχ ουτως.
Ex 10 5: הנשארת: G: το καταλειφθεν // ο κατελιπεν.
Lev 14 48: לא פשה: G: ου διαχυσει // ου διαχειται.

§ 6. COMBINATION OF TRANSLATION AND TRANSLITERATION.

Cf. *JBL*, 1935, 83, paragraph III: in both cases listed there, codex B offers a translation of the Hebrew word in question.

Gen 22 13: בסבך: G: εν φυτω // σαβεκ; cf. *TRL*, s. v. סבך.
Nu 25 15: אמות: G: εθνους // ομμουθ.
Gen 19 38: בן עמי: G: αμμαν // ο υιος του γενους μου. The transliterator apparently read עמון in his Hebrew text.

§ 7. THE DOUBLET GOES BACK TO A TRANSLATOR'S MISTAKE.

a. *Phonetic confusion.*

Gen 13 14: אתה: G: νυν // συ; cf. ib. 26 29: אתה עתה: G: και νυν συ. On the phonetic similarity of א and ע cf. *TRL*, paragraphs XI, XII, and XXIII under א and ע; *HPT*, § 3.
Gen 28 18: שם: G: εθηκεν // εκει; cf. Ex 15 25: שם שם: G: εκει εθετο. On the pronunciation of ש cf. *TRL*, paragraphs XIII and XIV; see also *HPT*, § 10.
Ex 10 4: ארבה: G: ακριδα // πολλην; this corresponds to MT and הרבה. On the interchangeability of א and ה, due to their pronunciation, cf. *TRL*, paragraphs XI, XII, and XXIII under א and ה; *HPT*, § 1.

b. *Graphic confusion.*

Gen 28 20: אם יהיה: G: εαν η // κυριος. This implies the reading of the Hebrew original once as יהיה (= MT), and once as יהוה; on the confusion between י and ו cf. *HPT*, § 30.

§ 8. TRANSLATION OF PARTICLES.

Lev 27 18: אחר: G: εσχατον // μετα.
Gen 38 1: עד: G: εως // προς.
Lev 27 18: עד: G: εως // εις.
Dt 31 6: עמך: G: μεθ υμων // εν υμιν; cf. Lev 25 45: עמכם: O': Vacat; al ex: μεθ υμων; *alia*: εν υμιν; cf. also Is 53 12: ואת פשעים נמנה: G: και εν τοις ανομοις ελογισθη, which is quoted Luke 22 37 as και μετα ανομων ελογισθη.

9. COMBINATION OF TWO TRANSLATIONS.

a. *Asyndetic connection.*

Gen 2 9: הדעת: G: του ειδεναι // γνωστον; cf. Ex 22 9: ראה: O': γνω; al ex: 'ιδη; Dt 29 2: ראו: O': εωρακασιν; al ex: ειδον; Ex 33 16: יודע: G: γνωστον εσται.
Gen 48 16: לרב: G: εις πληθος // πολυ.
Ex 1 9: רב: μεγα // πληθος; cf. Gen 45 28: רב: G: μεγα; Ex 19 21: רב: G: πληθος.
Ex 28 6: מעשה חשב: G: εργον υφαντου // ποικιλτου; cf. the rendering of מעשה חשב by G in Ex 26 1 as εργασια υφαντου; ib. 26 31 as εργον υφαντον; and ib. 28 15 as εργον ποικιλτου.
Ex 28 33: רמני: G: ωσει εξανθουσης ροας // ροισκους.
Ex 28 34: פעמן זהב: G: παρα ροισκον [χρυσουν // κωδωνα; cf. verse 33 below under b.
Ex 30 8: תמיד: G: ενδελεχισμου // δια παντος; cf. the translation of תמיד in Ex 29 42; Nu 28 6: G: ενδελεχισμου; but Ex 27 20, 28 30: G: δια παντος.
Ex 35 6: ותולעת שני: G: κοκκινον διπλουν // διανενησμενον; cf. the rendering of this Hebrew phrase by G in Ex 25 4: κοκκινον διπλουν, and Ex 28 8: κοκκινον διανενησμενου.

Lev 8 5: זה הדבר : G: τουτο εστιν το ρημα // τουτο εστιν. The literal translation of דבר by ρημα is characteristic for the asterisk-type of the Hexaplaric Septuagint; cf. Gen 20 10; Ex 18 14: הדבר הזה : O': ※ το ρημα ◟ τουτο; Gen 37 14; Josh 21 43: דבר : O': ※ ρημα ◟.

Dt 8 4: ורגלך : G: τα υποδηματα σου // οι ποδες σου.

b. *Connected by* και.

Gen 27 45: אף : G: τον θυμον // και την οργην; cf. Gen 49 6: באפם: G: εν τω θυμω αυτων; ib. verse 7: אפם : G: ο θυμος αυτων; but Gen 39 19: אפו : G: οργη.

Ex 15 18: לעולם : G: τον αιωνα // και επ αιωνα.

Ex 22 16: מאן ימאן : G: ανανευων ανανευση // και μη βουληται.

Ex 28 33: ופעמני זהב : G: το αυτο ειδος ροισκους χρυσους // και κωδωνας; cf. verse 34 above under a.

Ex 33 6: עדים : G: τον κοσμον αυτων // και την περιστολην; cf. verse 5 above X, § 8 c β 2 ב.

Lev 23 40: וערבי : G: και ιτεας // και αγνου κλαδου.

Dt 3 24: את גדלך : G: την ισχυν σου // και την δυναμιν σου; cf. την ισχυν μου in G Ex 9 16, quoted in Rom 9 17 as την δυναμιν μου.

c. *The two translations separated from one another.*

Bearing in mind that doublets originate in marginal glosses, which were included in the text by later copyists (cf. X § 7), we shall explain the following instances as inclusions at the wrong place; cf. similar misplacements Lev 13 37 in § 10 and Ex 12 5 above in X, § 8 e β 1.

Gen 15 13: וענו אתם : G: **και κακωσουσιν αυτο** ... // ... **και ταπεινωσουσιν αυτους**; cf. Gen 16 6: ותענה : G: **και εκακωσεν αυτην**; but ib. verse 9: והתעני : G: **και ταπεινωθητι**.

Ex 6 7: לי : G: εμαυτω // ... εμοι.

Ex 26 3: אשה אל אחתה (1°): G: ἐξ ἀλλήλων ...//... ἡ ἑτέρα ἐκ τῆς ἑτέρας; cf. ib. verse 6: אשה אל אחתה: G: ἑτέραν τῇ ἑτέρα.

Ex 26 12: תסרח... האהל בעדף ביריעת: G: τὸ πλεονάζον ἐν ταῖς δέρρεσιν τῆς σκηνῆς ... ὑποκαλύψεις ...//... τὸ πλεονάζον τῶν δέρρεων τῆς σκηνῆς ὑποκαλύψεις.

Lev 17 3, 4: או אשר ישחט מחוץ למחנה: ואל פתח אהל מועד לא הביאו להקריב קרבן ליהוה: G: καὶ ὃς ἂν σφάξῃ ἔξω τῆς παρεμβολῆς καὶ ἐπὶ τὴν θύραν τῆς σκηνῆς τοῦ μαρτυρίου μὴ ἐνέγκῃ ὥστε ποιῆσαι αὐτὸ εἰς ὁλοκαύτωμα ...//... καὶ ὃς ἂν σφάξῃ ἔξω καὶ ἐπὶ τὴν θύραν τῆς σκηνῆς τοῦ μαρτυρίου μὴ ἐνέγκῃ αὐτὸ ὥστε προσενέγκαι δῶρον κυρίου.

Nu 5 8: אליו: G: αὐτῷ ...//... πρὸς αὐτόν.

d. *Amalgamation of a doublet into one reading.*

In the following two cases I am inclined to see a fusion of two genuine translations, which were based upon corresponding Hebrew texts, the characteristic difference of which was their word-order with regard to the particle כל, cf. *HPT*, § 121, 4. Similar cases of such amalgamations see below in § 10 the instances from Lev 13 13 and Ex 25 23.

Gen 8 9: על פני כל הארץ: G: ἐπὶ παντὶ προσώπῳ πάσης τῆς γῆς. As basic readings I assume: 1. ἐπὶ προσώπῳ πάσης τῆς γῆς = MT; 2. ἐπὶ παντὶ προσώπῳ τῆς γῆς = על כל פני הארץ; cf. Gen 41 56: על כל פני הארץ: G: ἐπὶ προσώπου πάσης τῆς γῆς = על פני כל הארץ.

Ex 10 6: ובתי כל מצרים: G: καὶ πᾶσαι αἱ οἰκίαι ἐν πάσῃ γῇ τῶν αἰγυπτίων. I divide this pleonasmus (πᾶσαι ... πάσῃ) in: 1. καὶ αἱ οἰκίαι ἐν πάσῃ γῇ τῶν αἰγυπτίων = MT; 2. καὶ πᾶσαι αἱ οἰκίαι ἐν τῇ γῇ τῶν αἰγυπτίων = וכל בתי מצרים. We are here concerned solely with the word-order; hence, the question whether γῇ τῶν αἰγυπτίων really corresponds to MT מצרים, or rather to ארץ מצרים, and whether we should not read τῇ γῇ instead of γῇ (haplography), is at present of no importance.

§ 10. THE DOUBLET REFLECTS HEBREW VARIAE LECTIONES.

Ex 8 2: ותעל הצפרדע: G: και ανηγαγεν τους βατραχους // και ανεβιβασθη ο βατραχος. The Hebrew equivalents are: וַיַּעַל הַצְפַרְדֵּעַ (the verb in the *hiph'il*, the noun an object in the accusative) and MT.

Ex 26 5: אשה אל אחתה: G: αλληλαις // εις εκαστην; this corresponds to: MT and אִשָּׁה אֶל אֲחֹתָהּ.

Ex 28 20: משבצים זהב: G: περικεκαλυμμενα χρυσιω // συνδεδεμενα εν χρυσιω. This is equivalent to מְשֻׁבָּצִים זָהָב and MT.

Lev 7 3: ואת החלב המכסה את הקרב: G: και παν το στεαρ το κατακαλυπτον τα ενδοσθια // και παν το στεαρ το επι των ενδοσθιων. A combination of ואת כל החלב המכסה את הקרב and ואת כל החלב אשר על הקרב.

Lev 13 13: וטהר את הנגע: G: και καθαριει αυτον ο ιερευς // την αφην. This is a fusion of two translations: 1. και καθαριει αυτον ο ιερευς = וְטִהַר אֹתוֹ הַכֹּהֵן, and 2. και καθαριει την αφην = MT.

Lev 13 37: בעיניו: G: επωπιον // ... επι χωρας. The first translation = MT; επι χωρας = תַּחְתָּיו; cf. ib. verse 23: תחתיה: G: κατα χωραν. On the misplacement of the doublet cf. above § 9.

Nu 28 23: הבקר: G: της δια παντος // της πρωινης. The first translation = הַתָּמִיד; the second = MT.

Dt 4 20: ממצרים: G: εκ γης αιγυπτου // ... εξ αιγυπτου. A combination of מארץ מצרים and MT.

Ex 25 23: שלחן עצי שטים: G: τραπεζαν χρυσην // χρυσιου καθαρου. The two genuine translations presumably were: 1. τραπεζαν χρυσην = שֻׁלְחַן זָהָב, and 2. τραπεζαν χρυσιου καθαρου = שֻׁלְחַן זָהָב טָהוֹר; cf. § 9 d.

§ 11. GENERAL RESULTS.

Within certain limits the results we arrived at in X, § 9, while summing up the classification of the doublets in the Hexaplaric LXX quotations, hold true for the present groups of Pentateuch-doublets in Codex B and Codex A, too:

1. The doublets represent a combination of
   a) a translation and a transliteration (cf. X § 9 no. 2 a), or
   b) two translations of the Hebrew original (cf. ib. no 2 b)
2. In one case (Ex 34 15; cf. § 2 b) both sources could be traced, in quotations under O' and al ex, respectively (cf. X § 8 a). In a number of further instances (§ 2 a) the obelus text could be established as one of the sources (cf. X § 8 c). Bearing in mind our statement in X § 9, no. 6 we shall not hesitate to assign the still unidentified translation in § 2 a to the asterisk group.
3. When the doublet is formed by the combination of a literal and a free translation (cf. § 4), our remarks in XI b concerning the slavishly literal character of the asterisk type of the Hexaplaric LXX furnish us with a clue for assigning the components of these doublets to their respective sources.
4. As transliterations forming one part of a LXX doublet (above no. 1 a) we have to consider
   a) direct transliterations: Hebrew words which are still preserved in Greek spelling (§ 6); and
   b) indirect transliterations: Greek variants, which cannot be explained otherwise than as originating in a phonetic confusion of the basic Hebrew word (§ 7 a). The translators must have had the word in question before them in Greek transliteration.
5. While preparing their respective basic Greek texts which form the sources for the doublets, the original translators had their Hebrew originals before them; only thus confusions of letters on the ground of their similarity in the Hebrew alphabet could occur (cf. § 7 b, see also X, § 9, no. 4 a); the existence of phonetic confusions (cf. § 7 a) must, therefore, not be misconstrued as proving a translation upon mere dictation of the Hebrew text.

XIII. CODICES B AND A ON JUDGES.

In his *Septuaginta Studien*, Erster Teil, Goettingen 1891, Paul de Lagarde writes (p. 3) "Im Jahre 1705 erschien zu Oxford Johann Ernst Grabes *Epistola ad Joannem Millium*, der Professor der Theologie and Principal of Sanct Edmunds Hall war, 'qua ostenditur, libri Judicum genuinam LXX interpretum versionem eam esse, quam ms. codex alexandrinus exhibet, romanam autem editionem, quod ad dictum librum, ab illa prorsus diversam, atque eandem cum hesychiana esse'." Since the Roman edition of the LXX (editio Sixtina, Rome 1587) is based upon codex B (cf. Swete, *Introduction*, p. 181), Grabe's statement means that as far as the book of Judges is concerned, the codices B and A differ so widely from one another that while the latter represents the genuine LXX, codex B must necessarily reflect the recension of Hesychius (cf. above VI). Grabe indicated the reason, why he considers the text of codex A as the "genuine LXX," and not that of codex B by saying "libri Judicum versionem των O', quam Origenes in Hexaplis exhibuit, quaque omnes fere Christianorum ecclesiae post iudaicam synagogam olim usae sunt, et orientales hodie utuntur, codice alexandrino contineri deprehendi" (quoted by Lagarde, ib.).

Inspired by Grabe, Lagarde set out to investigate the relationship of the texts which these two manuscripts exhibit on the book of Judges: "Es handelte sich fuer Grabe, und handelt sich zunaechst auch fuer uns darum, den Text des Alexandrinus und den des Vaticanus, in Siglen A und B, gegen einander abzuschaetzen. Diese Abschaetzung kann nicht erfolgen, wenn nicht beide Gestaltungen des "Septuaginta"-texts vollstaendig einander gegenuebergestellt werden; die Lesarten des Einen unter dem Abdrucke des Andern anzugeben hilft kaum dem, der sich Jahre lang mit Septuagintastudien beschaeftigt hat, Anfaengern hilft es gewiss nicht. Es muss auch der Wert der Abschriften jener zwei Gestalten des "Septuaginta"-texts dargelegt werden: darum bessere ich die Fehler und Versehen der Abschreiber in meinem Abdrucke nicht. ... Es handelt sich darum, den Text von A und B einander gegenueber zu setzen, und diejenigen Zeugen fuer sie anzufuehren, die fuer den Beweis von Belang sind" (Lagarde, ib. 5).

As a specimen Lagarde published chapters I–V of Judges in such a way that each two pages form a unit: the left page brings the text of A and the right one that of B; both texts are provided with ample critical notes, listing the variant readings of either genuine Greek sources, or of translations based thereon. Thus, the sigla a c d h k p x ל ס indicate the witnesses of the A-text, while b g n ט p signify the B-group. The chief results of this study are formulated as follows: "Das Vorstehende [scil. the publication of the first five chapters of Judges in the indicated manner] genuegt, um folgende Thesen zu stellen: 1. Die im Codex A . . . stehende Uebersetzung des Buches der Richter stimmt im Grossen und Ganzen . . . mit dem Texte des Origenes. . . . 2. Codex B liefert nicht Varianten zu A, sondern enthaelt . . . eine andere Uebersetzung des Buches der Richter. Aus B in A, oder aus A in B hinueberkorrigieren darf nur der besonders Kundige und Besonnene" (ib. 71 f.).

Though published half a century ago, this procedure still enjoys a following. Alfred Rahlfs in his *Septuaginta* (Stuttgart, 1935) gives for the book of Judges the texts of both A and B in full. But a critical re-examination of Lagarde's premises and conclusions will show that what fifty years ago may have been a new and startling theory has lost its convincing power by now.

In order to arrive at definite conclusions concerning the relation of Codex A to the text of Origen's LXX, we have to bear in mind that our knowledge of the fifth column of Origen's *Hexapla* is based only upon citations. While arranging his large collections according to the order of the books in the OT, Field headed them by the symbol O', or by indicating: *alia exemplaria. Readings under either of these headings must be considered as reflecting Origen's LXX.* They differ from one another to such an extent as to suggest that they go back to two different translations, but this fact does not justify our arbitrarily regarding one of these readings as the "genuine" LXX of Origen, and rejecting the other. On the contrary, the only conclusion to be drawn must be that no "genuine" LXX (in the singular!) existed in Origen's days, but two independent translations of the Bible into Greek, both of which held an equal claim to be called "Septuagint." For the designation of one reading as O' and of the other as merely al ex is not given to them by Origen himself, nor is it to be explained from the nature of their sources; this is only a *Notbehelf* of the editor, and does not imply any difference in their authority as representing Origen's LXX.

With the way thus cleared for understanding Origen's work, we now proceed to an examination of the quotations from the fifth column and their relation to the two codices B and A. We extend our investigation concerning Codex A to include Codex B, too, since we wish to assign to both of them their respective place in the Hexaplaric LXX tradition. All our quotations are taken from the book of Judges in Field's *Hexaplorum quae supersunt*. In parentheses I indicate the symbol of that codex which offers the identical reading in his text.

1 1: ביהוה: O': δια του κυριου (=B); al ex: εν κυριω (=A).
1 1: בו ... אל הכנעני: O': προς τους χαναναιους ... προς αυτους (=B); al ex: προς τον χαναναιον ... εν αυτω (=A).
1 3: ונלחמה בכנעני: O': και παραταξωμεθα προς τους χαναναιους (=B); al ex: και πολεμησωμεν εν τω χαναναιω (=A, with the only difference that A reads πολεμησω, apparently a haplography before εν).
1 10: לפנים: O': το προτερον (=B); al ex: εμπροσθεν (=A).
1 11: וילך: O': και ανεβησαν (=B); al ex: επορευθησαν (=A).
1 14: בבואה: O': εν τη εισοδω αυτης (=B); al ex: εν τω εισπορευεσθαι αυτην (=A).
1 14: ותצנח מעל החמור: O': και εγογγυζεν και εκραζεν απο του υποζυγιου (=B, with the slight variant: εκραξεν); al ex: και εγογγυζεν επανω του υποζυγιου και εκραζεν απο του υποζυγιου (=A, also with the variant εκραξεν).
1 16: O': ιοθορ (=B); al ex: ιωβαβ (cf. A: ιωαβ).
1 16: חתן: O': του γαμβρου (=B); al ex: πενθερου (=A).
1 16: את בני: O': μετα των υιων (=B); al ex: προς τους υιους (=A).
1 17: חרמה: O': αναθεμα (=B); al ex: εξολοθρευσις (=A).

The result is that generally speaking B agrees with the quotations listed under O', and A with those under al ex. With the conclusions as formulated in X, § 6 in mind, we can formulate this result as follows: B reflects the obelus group, and A the asterisk group of the LXX on the book of Judges. Both must, therefore, be considered as reflecting the "genuine" LXX.

In making this statement we wish to emphasize that we do

not mean to imply that these codices represent the respective group in all their details. This is a problem which requires a careful and more detailed examination of at least considerable portions of the book of Judges. But since we do not aim at an exhaustive treatment of any of the problems discussed here, we might as well avail ourselves of this opportunity to state that we have reason to believe that the LXX texts as offered in either of these codices are the results of a long history of inner Greek development and adjustment to one another. We wish to demonstrate this assertion with a few examples:

1 6: וירדפו: O': και κατεδραμον (= B and A); al ex: και κατεδιωξαν.
1 7: ויביאהו: O': και αγουσιν αυτον (= B and A); al ex: και ηγαγον αυτον.
1 10: קרית ארבע: O': καριαθαρβοκ ÷ σεφερ ⨯ (cf. B: καριαρβοξε-φερ; A: καριαρβοκσεφερ); al ex: καριαθαρβοκ εξ εφραιμ.
2 10: נאספו: O': προσετεθησαν (= B and A); al ex: συνηχθησαν.
2 17: אחרים: O': ετερων (= B and A): al ex: αλλοτριων.
3 7: את הבעלים: O': τοις βααλιμ (cf. B: τοις βααλειμ; A: ταις βααλειμ) ; al ex: τη βααλ.
3 16: גמד: O': σπιθαμης (= B and A); al ex: δρακος.

In these instances the agreement between B and A in their readings will have to be explained as the result of an adjustment of A to the obelus text of B; for elsewhere A follows the asterisk text of al ex. Consequently, J. E. Grabe's statement "libri Iudicum versionem τῶν O', quam Origenes in Hexaplis exhibuit, ... codice alexandrino contineri deprehendi," the correctness of which Lagarde believed to have proven on the basis of his publication of the first five chapters of Judges, becomes now null and void. For in any agreement between O' and A we shall now see only the resultant of a later development of the text which was originally underlying A. This was achieved by way of eliminating some of the basic characteristics of the text which it had in common with the asterisk group.

This development must have taken place at a time when the obelus type had already gained increased authority at the expense of the asterisk type. We are inclined to see in this adjustment of A to the obelus type an effort to co-ordinate the A text with that textual form which had more or less become *the established text*; and that may also be the reason, why we could thus far discover no traces of a textual adjustment in the other direction, in order to bring about an agreement between B and the asterisk type, as represented by A. The asterisk type had lost ground to the obelus type!

We now return to Lagarde's publication of Judges 1–5 by putting in juxtaposition A and B with their respective critical apparatus. Our contention is that this procedure leads to no end: the texts of the various manuscripts which have been used by Lagarde for the preparation of the two critical apparatus, are already of a mixed type to such an extent that their assignment to either B or A must be considered as highly arbitrary. I will prove this by showing that

1. the critical apparatus on A equals that on B;
2. variant readings on the A text lead up to the respective readings of the B text; and vice versa
3. variants on B lead up to the A text.

1. *The critical apparatus on A lists the same readings as that on B.*

A hyphen separates here the symbols used by Lagarde to indicate the textual witnesses for the respective text; on the left side of the hyphen I bring the symbols for the A type; on the right side those for the B type:

1 1: $\epsilon\pi\eta\rho\omega\tau\eta\sigma\alpha\nu$ k א — n
1 6: $\epsilon\lambda\alpha\beta o\sigma\alpha\nu$ c d p x — b n
1 7: $\eta\gamma\alpha\gamma o\nu$ c d h k p א ס — n
1 8: $o\iota$ A c d h k p x Euseb: > a — B g n: > b
1 8: $\mu\alpha\chi\alpha\iota\rho\alpha s$ A — n
1 9: $\tau o\nu$ A: > a c d h k p x Euseb — B g n: > b
1 10: $\tau o\nu$ $\vartheta o\lambda\mu\iota$ c d א — g
1 11: beide Male $\delta\alpha\beta\iota\rho$ c — b beide Male
1 12: $\alpha\nu$ > h — g
1 12: vor $\delta\omega\sigma\omega$+$\kappa\alpha\iota$ x — g n

2. *Variants on A lead up to the textual readings of B.*

1 1: πολεμησαι a c d h k p x ℵ ▯ = B
1 2: εν τη χειρι k = B
1 3: και παραταξωμεθα προς τους χαναναιους ℵ = B
1 4: εκοψαν x = B
1 4: βεξεκ c d h k p x ℵ = B
1 5: κατελαβον x = B
1 8: ρομφαιας a c d h k p = B
1 9: την ορεινην a p = B
1 10: nach κατοικουντα+εν χεβρων a c d k p x ℵ ▯ = B
1 10: vor εξ+και εξηλθε χεβρων a d h p ℵ ▯ = B

3. *Variants on B lead up to the textual readings of A.*

1 1: προς τον χαναναιον g n = A
1 1: εν αυτω g n = A
1 2: τη > b g n = A
1 3: προς συμεων τον αδελφον g = A
1 3 και γε εγω g = A
1 5: vor φερεξαιον+τον g n = A
1 10: το δε g = A
1 10: χεβρων ην g = A
1 10: επαταξε n = A
1 12: αν b n = A

XIV. CODICES B AND A ON THE BIBLE.

In commenting upon J. E. Grabe's statement concerning the deviation of the LXX text on Judges as offered in Codex A from that in Codex B (see the preceding chapter at the beginning), Lagarde emphasized in a manner which is characteristic for him: "Die vielen Schnueffler mache ich darauf aufmerksam, dass Grabes Ausdruck 'quod ad dictum librum' die Untersuchung auf das Buch der Richter beschraenkt. Auch ich rede zunaechst nur von dem Buche der Richter" (*Septuaginta Studien*, 3).

The question as to whether the results obtained in the discussion of the book of Judges may be considered generally valid for these two manuscripts, or are applicable to this particular Biblical book only, has thus been left open. We, therefore, wish to take up this problem now. As a basis for our discussion we bring a few examples, which are taken at random from different parts of the Bible:

1. Codex B has the Hexaplaric readings under O';
Codex A those under al ex:

Hos 1 2: בהושע: O': εν ωσηε (=B); al ex: προς ωσηε (=A).
Hos 1 7: בסוסים: O': ουδε εν ιπποις (=B); al ex: praemittit: ουδε εν αρμασιν (=A).
Hos 2 25: ורחמתי את לא רחמה: O': και αγαπησω την ουκ ηγαπημενην (=B); al ex: και ελεησω την ουκ ελεημενην (=A).
Hos 6 6: ולא זבח: O': η θυσιαν (=B); al ex: και ου θυσιαν (=A).
Hos 13 3: וכעשן מארבה: O': και ως ατμις απο δακρυων (=B); al ex: και ως ατμις εκ καπνοδοχης (=A).

This last example is highly instructive. According to the text common to O' and B, the verse reads: "and like smoke from tears." This is sheer nonsense! It is quite possible that tears come as a result of smoke, but never does smoke originate in tears. δακρυων is an obvious error for ακριδων (cf. the reading noted in Field under *alia*: απο ακριδων), which goes back to a pronunciation of the basic Hebrew word מארבה as מָאַרְבָּה; cf. *JBL*, 1935, 82, paragraph II. The fact that O' and B share this error proves their interdependence.

Ezek 3 5: עמקי שפה וכבדי לשון: O': βαθυγλωσσον (=B); al ex: βαθυχειλον και βαρυγλωσσον (=A).
I Sam 1 1: צופים: O': σιφα (=B); al ex: σωφιμ (=A).
I Sam 1 1: ירחם: O': ιερεμεηλ (=B); al ex: ιεροαμ (=A).
I Sam 1 1: אפרתי: O': εφραιμ (=B); al ex: εφραθαιος (=A).
I Sam 1 3: האיש ההוא: O': ο ανθρωπος (=B); al ex: ο ανθρωπος εκεινος (=A).³
I Sam 1 4: ולכל בניה ובנותיה: O': και τοις υιοις αυτης (=B); al ex: και τοις υιοις αυτης και ταις θυγατρασιν αυτης (=A).

I Sam 1 13: רק שפתיה: O': και τα χειλη αυτης (=B); al ex: πλην τα χειλη αυτης (=A).

Ps 103 2: גמוליו: O': τας αινεσεις (=B); al ex: τας ανταποδοσεις (=A).

Ps 104 18: לשפנים: O': τοις χοιρογρυλλιοις (=B); al ex: τοις λαγωοις (=A). On the unique importance of this passage cf. *Festschrift Kahle*, 43 ff.

2. Words missing in O' and B, but quoted under al ex and contained in A:

Ezek 3 9: נתתי מצחך: O': Vacat. (missing in B); al ex: δεδωκα το νικος σου (=A).

Ezek 6 9: אל הרעות אשר עשו: O': Vacat. (missing in B); al ex: ※ περι των κακιων ων εποιησαν ✕ (=A).

I Sam 1 9: ואחרי שתה: O': Vacat. (missing in B); al ex: και μετα το πιειν (=A).

I Sam 1 11: לא תשכח את אמתך: O': Vacat. (missing in B); al ex: και μη επιλαθη της δουλης σου (=A).

These examples seem to suggest that the results at which we arrived in the preceding chapter with regard to B and A on Judges, may well be applied in general to the interrelation of these two manuscripts as such. We can not base any final theories on our findings; in order to arrive at well-founded conclusions, we should have to make first a thorough examination of each book separately; and this we did not do. We therefore stress the tentative nature of our suggestion, namely: that after having investigated considerable portions of the Bible we find a striking interrelation between the obelus type of the Hexaplaric LXX and Codex B on one side, and between the asterisk type and Codex A on the other side. Further examination makes it plausible that here, too, the later adjustment of the basic texts of these manuscripts followed a tendency of discarding the asterisk type of Codex A, in order to bring it under the influence of the obelus type, by eliminating asterisk readings and substituting readings from the obelus group in their stead. This procedure thus leads to an agreement between the readings under O', B and A, as against the respective al ex readings:

Hos 1 4: יהוא: O': ιουδα (=B and A); al ex: ιηου.
Hos 4 4: ועמך: O': ο δε λαος μου (=B and A); al ex: ο δε λαος σου.
Hos 4 5: עמך: O': μετα σου (=B and A); al ex: μετ αυτου.
Hos 5 13: לרפא: O': ιασασθαι (=B and A); al ex: ρυσασθαι.
Ezek 3 18: בעונו: O': τη αδικια αυτου (=B and A); al ex: τη ανομια αυτου.
Ezek 4 2: סללה: O': χαρακα (=B and A); al ex: ταφρον.

In conclusion we may, therefore, say that taking the codices B and A as entities, the divergencies displayed therein largely reflect similar variant readings of the two types of the Hexaplaric LXX; thus, B shows close affinity to the obelus type, and A to the asterisk type. Neither of them can be regarded as representing their respective basic textual type in all its details; the very fact that the text of either manuscript is of a mixed type, precludes any such assumption. Byt, still, though no absolute classification of these manuscripts is possible, we may say that relatively speaking B has better preserved its original characteristics of the obelus type than A its of the asterisk type, since we saw a tendency of bringing B and A into agreement at the expense of A.

Cautiously as these conclusions are phrased, they are of the utmost significance for the solution of our problem. Until now we had merely evidence for the former existence of an obelus type of the LXX, but no coherent text of it to point to. We could establish certain characteristics of this text, but its very existence was a matter of conjecture, since it was based on fragmentary quotations only. Now we have in Codex B a coherent manuscript, covering nearly all of the Bible, which may rightly be classified as a direct offspring of the obelus type, exhibiting the readings of this type to an extraordinarily large extent.

We are now confronted with the problem: Can we prove in the same or in some similar way the existence of a coherent text of the asterisk type, evidence for which we possess up to now solely in the form of citations? The next chapter will deal with the solution of this problem.

D. THE CHURCH FATHERS AND VETUS LATINA

XV. THE MINOR PROPHETS IN GREEK.

What we have attained thus far in our search for coherent Bible texts in Greek as representatives of either of the two Hexaplaric types of the LXX shows that while Codex B might be considered as a witness for the obelus type, the undoubtedly asterisk character underlying Codex A has already undergone too great changes for that MS to be rated a genuine asterisk text now. We therefore turn to the Early Christian writers in the hope of finding some pertinent information in their commentaries on the Bible. It is good to remind ourselves at the very outset that our expectations must not be too high; for the same levelling hand which we noticed at work in Codex A, busy to substitute the more authoritative obelus text for its former asterisk readings, no doubt extended its influence even beyond this manuscript, so as to include Church Father commentaries, too. In those early centuries the Church Fathers' works exercized a great influence in the religious life of Christendom; what good was it, then, to copy such commentaries with references to a Bible text which did not fully agree with the authoritative Bible of the Church? The readings had to be changed, and actually were changed. Corrections of this kind are surely *bona fide* emendations; but the resulting readings are worthless for us. For we realize that any such agreement in the Church Fathers' commentaries with the obelus text might possibly be — though it certainly is not always — the outgrowth of scribal changes. Consequently, we shall value so much higher those deviations from the obelus text in the Church Father literature which obviously escaped the attention of their respective copyists, and remained uncorrected. Evidence of this kind cannot be properly appreciated by merely counting the number of the text-witnesses for a certain reading; but each instance has to be taken *by weight and not by count*.

We have further to bear in mind that, since we established two textual types for the Hexaplaric LXX, we now always need two deviating texts of the same Biblical passage, so as to assign even one of them to the asterisk or obelus type. Now the criteria by which we proceed are very scarce. If we are about to establish the basic type of a given text we must look in Field's Hexapla for quotations from the same Biblical book listed both under O′ *and* al ex. A mere O′ quotation — as is the vast majority of cases in Field's work — is of no avail; in the agreement between our text and such O′ quotations we can not see a proof for the obelus type of our text so long as we have no evidence that the asterisk type had this same passage in a different phrasing. We therefore can base our investigation solely upon a comparison of two divergent readings: be they represented by an O′ quotation and a corresponding al ex variant reading, as was our procedure till now, or else by two other different coherent texts covering a substantial part of a Biblical book, provided the differences are genuine (cf. our characterizations in X § 9 and XII § 11) and not the apparent result of later inner Greek textual development (cf. below under V).

We can point to one case which meets with these requirements: the Minor Prophets, as commented upon by Cyril of Alexandria and by Theodoret of Kyros. In an article "The Problems of the Septuagint Recensions," *JBL*, 1935, 73–92, I published the results of an examination of the Greek Bible texts, which served these Fathers as bases for their commentaries. The variant readings are grouped and classified; they prove that these two Fathers used two different Bible texts in Greek, which in turn go back to two independent translations of the Hebrew Minor Prophets into Greek. This is demonstrated by referring to variant readings which cannot be explained otherwise but as reflecting a different approach to the basic Hebrew text. Differences of such a type may be seen in a translation which is based upon a mispronunciation of the Hebrew word or a mistake on account of the similarity in the script of certain Hebrew letters. They may be used as evidence for the fact that the translator was rather poorly equipped for his task, and thus account for so many other errors. But they are, from the viewpoint of the philologian, the most trustworthy evidence for an assertion that this text with all its mistakes is really an independent translation, based upon a Hebrew original, and not a mere stylistic revision of an already existent Greek translation.

We thus have very large portions of the Minor Prophets in Greek in a twofold shape: that of Cyril and that of Theodoret. How do they compare with our division into asterisk and obelus type?

This question can best be answered by referring to the variants themselves. I follow the order of my article in *JBL*, referring even to the respective headings; but I must leave out those instances for which we have no corresponding citations from the *Hexapla*. The Church Fathers I quote according to Migne's *Patrologia Graeca*; Cyril's commentary (here abbreviated into Cy) appears in vols. 71 and 72; that of Theodoret (here shortened to Th) in volume 81. In Migne's edition, every page is divided into four sections, which are indicated by the letters A, B, C, D. I use these with the page citation.

I. The Hebrew word is incorrectly spelled.

Hos 8 1: שפר חכך אל: O': εις κολπον αυτων ως γη = Cy (p. 197 B); al ex: επι φαρυγγι αυτων ως γη αβατος ως σαλπιγξ = Th (p. 1592 D).

Al ex contains this reading in addition to the O' reading; this means that it is a doublet, combining the O' reading and the Theodoret-text. Hence the text of Th appears to be older and better preserved than that of al ex.

Obadiah 16: ולעו: O': και καταβησονται = Cy (p. 592 B); al ex: και καταπιονται = Th (p. 1716 B).

Hab 3 12: תצעד: O': ολιγωσεις = Cy (p. 932 A); al ex: συμπατησεις = Th (p. 1832 B).

II. The Hebrew word is incorrectly vocalized.

Hos 13 3: וכעשן מארבה: O': και ως ατμις απο δακρυων = Th (p. 1621 D: απο ακριδων); al ex: και ως ατμις εκ καπνοδοχης = Th (p. 300 D: απο). On the inner Greek corruption of ακριδων as offered by Th, into δακρυων in O', cf. XIV 1.

Am 6 2: עברו כלנה: O': διαβητε παντες = Cy (p. 513 D); al ex: διαβητε εις χαλανην = Th (p. 1693 B). Here again, al ex has this reading in addition to the O' reading; cf. our remark above on Hos 8 1.

Zeph 1 5: במלכם: O': κατα του 'βασιλεως αυτων = Cy (p. 949 D); κατα του μελχομ = Th (p. 1840 C).

IV. Doublets in Theodoret.

Zech 6 7: ויבקשו: O': και επεβλεπον = Cy (p. 88 B); al ex: και εζητουν και επεβλεπον = Th (p. 1905 A).

Zech 7 3: הנזר: O': το αγιασμα = Cy (p. 100 C); al ex: το αγιασμα η νηστευσω = Th (p. 1908 B/C). The two translations are connected by η; cf. in X § 8 a β the instance from II Kg 1 30.

V. Greek corruptions in Theodoret.

Hos 4 19: אותה: O': συ ει = Cy (p. 137 D); al ex: συριει = Th (p. 1576 D). The original translator of συ ει read the Hebrew word as אַתָּה; but no connection can be traced between אותה and συριει (from συριζω = to whistle). It is very likely that the preceding πνευματος misled the copyist to seek in συ ει a verb which expresses some of the doings of the "wind," and thus guessed συριει for it.

Hos 9 10: כבכורה: O': ως σκοπον = Th (p. 1601 B); al ex: ως συκον = Cy (p. 229 B). Similarly in Nah 3 12: בכורים in rendered by Theodoret (p. 1805 B/C): σκοπους; how the same mistake could occur in both passages, I am unable to explain.

The last two examples do not count at all when we try to establish the textual types of Cyril's and Theodoret's Bibles. For they do not represent two independent translations (our main requirement), but only one, which appears correctly in one text but corrupt in the other. These corruptions must have been widespread, as becomes evident from the number of texts which have these readings; cf. Field a. l. Of course, this does not give additional importance to them; they remain corruptions, still. But it proves the interrelation of the texts which have these errors in common.

Similarly the two examples of doublets carry only little weight. They belong to that group which we would term "doublets of which one reading is traceable"; cf. X § 8 a δ and XII § 2 a. They are the result of a combination of the O' reading (which is identical with Cyril's text) with the reading of another genuine translation, which still remains to be discovered, and which, it may safely be assumed, preserved much better the basic textual type of al ex (i. e. Theodoret's text).

Speaking of doublets, mention must be made of the passages Hos 8 1 and Am 6 2 which are listed above. Here Cyril and Theodoret offer different readings, which prove the genuineness of their respective translation. Under al ex a. l. Field quotes readings, which are a combination of these two renderings. These doublets belong to the same type which we discussed in X § 8 a a. They prove that here the texts of Cyril and Theodoret are better preserved than that of al ex, since they still offer the original sources for the doublets of al ex. But they can not be used as evidence to determine the textual type of either of these Church Fathers.

But from the remaining examples it becomes clear that we may assign Cyril's text to the obelus type, and Theodoret's text to the asterisk type. We again emphasize that our conclusions concern themselves only with the basic character of the two texts in question, and do not preclude the existence of sporadic exceptions. Hos 13 3 seems to be such an exception; but the textual tradition is here confused to such an extent (cf. Field, where Theodoret's reading is listed as a third possibility under *alia*) that we prefer to refrain from commenting on this passage.

Cyril contains all of the Minor Prophets in Greek, Theodoret approximately one-third of the text, but as a more or less coherent text, and not as mere abrupt fragments of sentences, like the quotations in Field's collection. While Cyril is thus a welcome addition to our textual witnesses for the obelus group, we have in Theodoret now the first real text of the asterisk group, covering considerable portions of Biblical books. For further witnesses for the asterisk group we shall have to turn to indirect evidence, namely, the Latin translations of the LXX.

XVI. THE LXX IN LATIN.

Augustinus in his *De doctrina christiana* 2, 11 (quoted by Friedrich Stummer, *Einfuehrung in die lateinische Bibel*, Paderborn 1928, 51) states that the Latin translations of the Bible — scil. in the period prior to Jerome — were based upon Greek originals: "qui scripturas ex Hebraea lingua in Graecam verterunt, numerari possunt, Latini autem interpretes nullo modo; ut enim cuique primis fidei temporibus in manus venit codex Graecus et aliquantulum facultatis sibi utriusque linguae habere videbatur, ausus est interpretari." This statement clearly refers to those Latin Bible texts which were executed by Christians and meant for Christians, or at least for prospective Christians; the problem raised by D. S. Blondheim in his *Les parlers judéo-romans et la Vetus Latina* (Paris, 1925) whether the Latin speaking Jews of Gaul had a Bible of their own or not, will not concern us here.

Since the Latin Bible translations were based upon Greek originals, they might be used in restoring these originals by retroverting them into Greek. Such a procedure might help us regain an otherwise lost Greek text of the Bible, or at least of portions of it. Accordingly, in *MGWJ*, 1937, 55–65 I published a translation into Greek of an Old Latin text of the book of Ruth. As a result of this procedure I arrived at the conclusion that "Durch die vorangehende Rueckuebersetzung erhalten wir *nicht* eine neue griechische *Handschrift* des Buches Ruth — der Gewinn waere nicht gar so gross, wenn man bedenkt, dass schon Holmes and Parsons, und spaeter Brooke and McLean 50 Handschriften fuer ihre Ausgaben kollationierten!—, sondern eine neue, bisher sonst *unbekannte griechische Textgestalt* dieses Buches, *die auf eine von der landlaeufigen Septuaginta unabhaengige Uebersetzung des Buches Ruth ins Griechische zurueckgeht*" (ib. 63).

We are thus building upon the foundation laid out by Augustin that these Old Latin texts go back to respective Greek texts, and reflect only indirectly a Hebrew text. Can we prove the correctness of Augustin's statement from the very Latin texts themselves? Inner evidence deserves more credence than mere tradition handed down by early authors, as we could see in our analysis of Origen's work on the fifth column of the *Hexapla*.

Variant readings, which do or do not coincide with MT, are not conclusive at all. For such variants might just as well be explained as having their origin in a corresponding Greek prototype of the Latin text, as in a basic Hebrew text; since they lend themselves to a retroversion into both languages, it could be argued either way. "Ich glaube nun, dass dies Problem auf Grund solcher Stellen zu loesen ist, die in ihrem Zusammenhange sinnlos sind, aber durch Vornahme einer kleinen Korrektur verstaendlich werden" (*MGWJ*, 1937, 64). As long as we have to go back to the Hebrew text in order to explain such a mistake, we shall consider this Hebrew text to be the direct original of the translation in question. But in case the Hebrew phrase could by no errors in its pronunciation or etymology lead to the confusion in the Latin text, while the equivalent Greek phrase could, we shall see herein a proof of the dependence of the Latin text upon this Greek text as its basic original. In my article in *MGWJ* I demonstrated this by referring to Ruth 3 10: "*ut inires post iubenes* steht in offenem Widerspruch zu 2 21: *cum puellis meis adiunge te*: ib. 22: *quod existi cum puellis eius*; und ib. 23: *et adiunxisti te cum puellis booz*. Was Boaz also in 3 10 im Sinne hatte, war: *ne inires post iubenes*. Der Fehler erklaert sich aus einer griechischen Vorlage, in der in der Phrase: τοῦ μὴ πορευθῆναι σε das μὴ ausgefallen war. Das verbleibende τοῦ πορευθῆναι σε musste Lat. durch *ut inires* wiedergeben" (ib. 64).

A few more examples will make this point clearer: In Ruth 1 2 this Latin text reads: *et nomina erat duobus filiis eius*; the subject is a *neutrum pluralis*, the predicate a singular. This is a grammatical rule in Greek syntax only, not in Latin; consequently, the translator must have had: και ονοματα ην before him, and imitated this original exactly (cf. similar cases in the Aramaic Bible Version, *ZAW*, 1927, 279, paragraph XXI). In Ruth 1 11 we read: *redite filie mee ut quid uenistis mecum*. The corresponding Hebrew text has למה תלכנה עמי : future tense. For this speech was delivered *before* Naomi set out to return to Bethlehem in Judaea, and was meant to prevent her daughters-in-law from joining her. Her advice was accepted by Orfa; cf. verse 14: *et osculata est orfa socrum suam et habiit*; but Ruth stood firm in her decision to follow her mother-in-law; cf. verse 16: *ne obuiaberis mici ut relinquam te, ut revertar depost te*. Both women were thus advised in verse 11, *from now on* to part from their mother-in-law; the perfect tense of *uenistis* is, therefore, an apparent mistake for the corresponding future-form. By referring to a Greek original, the explanation is quite simple: ἱνα τι πορευεσϑε was misunderstood in ἱνα τι επορευεσϑε.

Thus inner criteria, as offered by this Latin text itself, substantiate the correctness of Augustin's assertion to the effect that the Vetus Latina is based upon Greek originals. Here the question arises: what textual type did these Greek originals represent? The Vetus Latina is said to originate in the second century C.E., this means about the time of Origen; consequently, the translators had the LXX before them in a twofold form: as the obelus and the asterisk types. Which of them was taken as the basis for their work? This problem is of importance from many points of view: if preference was consistently given by the translators to one and the same Greek type, it may be taken as an indication of its wider circulation and higher authority. In addition: by establishing relation of an interdependence between a Greek type and the Vetus Latina, we might hereafter utilize this Latin translation as a text witness for that Greek type upon which it is based.

Our procedure in such a case, based upon a *comparison of two texts*, is outlined in chapter XV. We need two parallel Latin texts and corresponding evidence from Origen in order to deal with this problem. Ernest Ranke published under the title *Par Palimpsestorum Wirceburgensium* (Vienna, 1871) fragments of original manuscripts containing Vetus Latina texts, for considerable portions of which he could bring in a parallel column another Old Latin version, referred to as "apud Augustinum, Hieronymum aliosve obvia." Jerome's "Vulgata nova," which Ranke publishes in a third column, does not interest us, since it is based on the Hebrew text. We thus have quite a number of chapters of various Biblical books in two Old Latin translations. A mere cursory examination reveals the existence of many variants between them. Do these variants represent two Latin possibilities of rendering one and the same Greek text into Latin (e. g. synonyms, stylistic polish), or do they reflect two corresponding Greek texts? Here, too, a seemingly hopeless confusion will furnish us with the clue.

Hos 4 19 צרר רוח אותה: the Vetus Latina according to the Wuerzburg fragment reads: *haec conuersio spiritus tu es*, thus reading or interpreting אותה as אַתָּה *tu es* (we purposely refer first to the Hebrew text as prototype as long as feasible). But the translation in the parallel column has: *turbo spiritus sibilabit* (Ranke, 249). Here the Hebrew word אותה is of no use; for the way from אותה to שרק or נשב is too long! Fortunately, we possess this passage in quotations from both types of the Hexaplaric LXX: cf. the preceding chapter sub V. Latin *tu es* could never be confused into sibilabit; but Greek συ ει into συριει could. Thus, al ex and the second Old Latin text share this mistake, which could originate only in Greek. We may, therefore, say: both the obelus and the asterisk types of the LXX were used as basic texts for retroversion into Latin, the so-called Vetus Latina; and a minute comparison of a given Old Latin text with the extant Greek material of the two LXX types is required, before we assign this Old Latin text to one type or the other.

We shall demonstrate this first on the book of Ruth in the Old Latin version:

a. Readings both under O' and under *alia exemplaria*.

1 1: בימי שפט: O': εν τω κρινειν (=B); al ex: εν ταις ημεραις του κρινειν = in diebus iudicis.

1 5: משני ילדיה ומאישה: O': απο του ανδρος αυτης και απο των δυο υιων αυτης (=B); al ex: απο των δυο υιων αυτης και απο του ανδρος αυτης = a duobus filiis suis et a uiro suo.

3 15: ואחזו בה ותאחז בה: O': και εκρατησεν αυτο (=B); al ex: και κρατησον αυτο και εκρατησεν αυτο = et tene eam et tenuit illam.

3 16: ותאמר מי את בתי: O': η δε ειπεν αυτη θυγατερ (=B); al ex: η δε ειπε τι εστι θυγατερ = et dixit quid est filia.

3 16: ותגד לה: O': και ειπεν αυτη (=B); al ex: και απηγγειλεν αυτη = et indicabit ei.

b. Readings *sub asterisco*.

1 1: ושני בניו: O': και οι ※ δυο ⸔ υιοι αυτου = et duo filii eius; cf. B: και οι υιοι αυτου.

1 22: כלתה עמה: O': η νυμφη αυτης ※ μετ αυτης ⸔ = nurus eius cum ea; cf. B: η νυμφη αυτης.

2 23: וקציר החטים: O': και ※ τον θερισμον ⸔ των πυρων = et messem frumentariam; cf. B: και των πυρων.

3 7: ויאכל בעז וישת: O': και εφαγε βοοζ ※ και επιε ⸔ = et manducabit booz et bibit; cf. B: και εφαγεν βοος.

3 7: וחשכב: O': Vacat. (missing in B, too); al ex: ※ και εκοιμηθη ⸔ = et dormibit.

We thus see that this Old Latin text belongs to the asterisk type; the agreement between the Hexaplaric asterisk type and this Old Latin version of Ruth includes: the actual amount of text (which on the other hand is missing in the obelus type), the choice of words, the word-order and the transliteration of Hebrew; on this last item (βοοζ — booz, as against βοος in B), cf. *TRL*, paragraph XXIII under r. By way of retroversion of this Latin text into Greek (*MGWJ*, 1937, 55 seq.) I restored the asterisk type of the LXX on Ruth, which together with B, representing the obelus type, make a *complete Hexaplaric book of Ruth in Greek*.

We shall now examine the two forms of Old Latin Bible translation as published in Ranke's book, with Field's *Hexapla* at hand, in order to note any interconnection. In parenthesis I indicate the page in Ranke, so as to make easy the locating of the passages. The first quotation in Latin refers to the Wuerzburg fragment; the second to the parallel source, according to Ranke.

a. Hexaplaric readings both under O' and al ex traceable in the Vetus Latina.

(p. 181): Ex 33 19: בשם יהוה: nomine meo dms = O': το ονοματι μου · κυριος; nomine Domini = al ex: τω ονοματι κυριου.

(p. 207) Lev 5 19: אשם אשם: negligentia = O': πλημμελεια; delicto delictum = al ex: πλημμελεια πλημμελησιν.

(p. 241) Hos 1 2: בהושע: in osee = O': ἐν ὡσηε; ad osee = al ex: πρὸς ὡσηε.
(p. 253) Hos 6 4: מה אעשה לך: quid tibi faciam = O': τι σοι ποιησω; quid faciam tibi = al ex: τι ποιησω σοι.
(p. 253) Hos 6 6: ולא זבח: quam sacrificium = O': ἡ θυσιαν; et non sacrificium = al ex: και ου θυσιαν.
(p. 321) Thr 3 23: חדשים לבקרים: et noua in matutinum = O': καινα εις τας πρωιας; renovabit illas sicut lux matutina = al ex: ανακαινισον αυτους ως ορθρον πρωιμον.
(p. 335) Ezek 34 27: את מטות עלם: torquam eorum = O': τον ζυγον αυτων; furcas iugi eorum = al ex: τους κλαιους του ζυγου αυτων.

On the reading: τον ζυγον του κλαιου αυτων, which Field also lists under al ex, cf. G on Ex 3 2: εν πυρι φλογος, quoted in Acts 7 30 as: εν φλογι πυρος; also G on Jer 18 6: ο πηλος του κεραμεως, quoted in Rom 9 21, as: ο κεραμευς του πηλου.

b. Readings *sub asterisco*, traceable with and without the asteriscized words.

(p. 258) Is 29 7: לילה:—;nocte = O': ※ νυκτος ⸓.
(p. 261) Is 29 13: בפיו:—; cf. O': Vacabat; ore suo = ※ εν τω στοματι αυτου ⸓.
(p. 296) Jer 22 28: הוא וזרעו:—; ipse et semen eius = O': ※ αυτος και το σπερμα αυτου ⸓.
(p. 325) Ezek 24 9: אוי עיר הדמים:—; cf. O': Vacat.; vae civitas sanguinum = ※ ουαι πολις των αιματων ⸓.
(p. 332) Ezek 34 16: ואת השמנה:—; cf. O': Vacat.; et quod pingue est = ※ και το πιον ⸓.

These observations may, therefore, lead to a conclusion that the Wuerzburg fragment of the Vetus Latina is closely related to the obelus type, while the other evidence for the Vetus Latina is in a similar way dependant on the asterisk type of the LXX. Thus we do not exclude the possibility that either text might at certain passages offer readings which reverse this relationship; for we already noticed that all the texts we had to deal with present themselves as belonging to an already mixed type. A few examples will show that the same is the case with the two Vetus Latina texts under examination:

(p. 177) Ex 32 24: ואשלכהו: et misi illud = O': και ερριψα ※ αυτα; et misi.

(p. 183) Ex 34 7: חסד: et facies misericordiam = al ex: και ποιων ελεος; et misericordiam = O': και ελεος.

(p. 293) Jer 22 14: האמר:—; cf. O': Vacat;—; but cf. ※ ο λεγων ⨯.

(p. 302) Jer 23 22: מדרכם הרע:—; —; but cf. ※ εκ της οδου αυτων της πονηρας και ⨯.

The difficulty which I experienced in trying to find these few instances to prove the mixed type of these two Latin texts, may also be taken as an indication that their basic character as representing the obelus and asterisk types, respectively, is still by far predominant.

We have thus succeeded in proving the existence of the two Hexaplaric LXX types also as coherent Bible texts, represented both in the Greek originals and in their Latin translations. The textual evidence for each one of these types as far as we could now trace them are:

1. The obelus type: Hexaplaric quotations under O' and *sub obelo*; Codex B of the LXX; Cyril of Alexandria on the Minor Prophets, the Vetus Latina according to the Wuerzburg fragment.

2. The asterisk type: Hexaplaric quotations under al ex and *sub asterisco*; Codex A of the LXX (to a certain extent only!); Theodoret of Kyros on the Minor Prophets; the book of Ruth according to the Vetus Latina, and one tradition within the Vetus Latina generally.

E. CONCLUSIONS

XVII. The NT and the Two LXX Types.

The starting point of our investigation was the stressing of the apparent incongruities between certain OT passages as quoted in the NT and the way they are worded at their respective places within the OT itself. These discrepancies resulted from a comparison of both, OT and NT according to one and the same manuscript, Codex B. Our presupposition here was that since this manuscript combines both Testaments into one complete Bible, we should be able to verify easily text-quotations from the OT in the NT, just as cross-references in one volume must refer to passages actually to be found there. But in the course of our re-examination of the ancient sources for our knowledge of the OT in Greek, we realized that there is no basis for the theory of Lagarde of an Archetypal LXX, implying that the OT in Greek was originally known and published in a single uniform type which only later developed into different recensions. On the contrary, we saw that as late as in the days of Origen two different translations of the OT into Greek were known as LXX. In combining their variant readings in the fifth column of his *Hexapla* he indicated the source, from which these variants came, by marking them with an obelus or asterisk, respectively. But the very fact that he incorporated these readings in the fifth column proves that he considered the two translations as genuine LXX.

We said that *as late* as the days of Origen the LXX was so to say the common denominator for two translations. This means that we have evidence to prove the existence of these translations at a period prior to that of Origen. To be exact, we have to limit ourselves to proving the existence of the asterisk type only (the obelus type was well represented throughout the centuries in codex B; cf. XIV towards the end); this translation must have been withdrawn from circulation not long after Origen and was then forgotten. We shall do this on the basis of the OT quotations in the NT, which differ from the text offered in Codex B. The number of all these passages combined represents merely a fraction of the total references to the OT as found in the NT, since their vast majority fully agree with Codex B. This in itself is a proof that the LXX type of Codex B, which as we said before is the obelus type, originates in a pre-Origenian period, since the authors of the NT quoted from it. But our concern here is only the asterisk type, the former existence of which has to be proven from the NT.

1. *OT quotations in the NT identical with readings under al ex.*

Rom 9 17: εις αυτο του εξηγειρα σε οπως ενδειξωμαι εν σοι τ η ν δ υ ν α μ ι ν μ ο υ; cf. Ex 9 16: את כחי: O': την ισχυν μου; al ex: την δυναμιν μου.

Rom 11 4: κατελειπον εμαυτω επτακισχιλιους ανδρας οιτινες ουκ εκαμψαν γονυ τη βααλ; cf. 1 Kg 19 18: לא כרעו: O': ουκ ωκλασαν γονυ; al ex: ουκ εκαμψαν γονυ.

Rom 9 33: ιδου τιθημι εν σιων λιθον προσκομματος και πετραν σκανδαλου κ α ι ο π ι σ τ ε υ ω ν ε π α υ τ ω ου καταισχυνθησεται; cf. Is 28 16: המאמין: O': και ο πιστευων; al ex: και ο πιστευων επ αυτω.

Luke 3 4, 5: φωνη βοωντος ... και εσται τ α σ κ ο λ ι α εις ευθειαν και αι τραχειαι ε ι s ο δ ο υ s λ ι α s; cf. Is 40 4: העקב: O': ÷ παντα ✕ τα σκολια; לבקעה: O': εις πεδια; al ex: εις οδους λειας.

Here the close affinity between the NT and the asterisk type of the OT becomes even more obvious by the fact that the obelus reading ÷ παντα ✕ is not included in this lengthy quotations; cf. similarly Matth 12 17, 18: ιδου ο παις μου ... ο αγαπητος μου, compared with Is 42 1: בחירי ... עבדי הן: O': ÷ ιακωβ ✕ ο παις μου ... ÷ ισραηλ ✕ ο εκλεκτος μου. Here, too, the two words *sub obelo* ÷ ιακωβ ✕ and ÷ ισραηλ ✕ are not contained in the NT quotation; cf. on the importance of this variant reading above III a 4.

Rom 3 10, 16, 17: ουκ εστιν δικαιος ... συντριμμα και ταλαιπωρια εν ταις οδοις αυτων και οδον ειρηνης ο υ κ ε γ ν ω σ α ν cf. Is 59 8: ולא ידעו: O': ουκ οιδασι; al ex: ουκ εγνωσαν.

Matth 9 13 and 12 7: ελεος θελω κ α ι ο υ θ υ σ ι α ν; cf. Hos 6 6: ולא זבח: O': η θυσιαν; al ex: και ου θυσιαν. See the discussion of this passage above III c.

Hebr 12 6: ον γαρ αγαπα κυριος π α ι δ ε υ ε ι; cf. Prov 3 12: יוכיח: O': ελεγχει; al ex: παιδευει.

Perhaps not quite as convincing as these passages, but still not less important for the establishing of a chronology of the texts involved, is:

SPERBER: NEW TESTAMENT AND SEPTUAGINT 281

Matth 26 31: παταξω τον ποιμενα και διασκορπισθησονται τα προβατα της ποιμνης; cf. Zech 13 7: הך את הרעה ותפוצין הצאן: O': παταξατε τους ποιμενας και εκσπασατε τα προβατα; al ex: παταξον τον ποιμενα και διασκορπισθησονται τα προβατα. The agreement between Matthew and al ex in the choice of the verb διασκορπισθησονται (as against εκσπασατε of O') suggests an interdependence of these two texts.

2. *NT quotations from the Minor Prophets identical with Theodoret's readings.*

Matth 9 13 and 12 7: ελεος θελω και ου θυσιαν; cf. Hos 6 6 according to Th (p. 1584 C): και ου θυσιαν, while Cy (p. 165 D) has: η θυσιαν. On the variant Th: ελεον — Cy: ελεος cf. *JBL*, 1935, 86, paragraph VIII.

Luke 23 30: τοτε αρξονται λεγειν τοις ορεσιν πεσετε εφ ημας και τοις βουνοις καλυψατε ημας; cf. Hos 10 8 according to Th (p. 1608 A/B); in Cy (p. 248 C) the word-order is changed.

Acts 2 18: καιγε επι τους δουλους μου και επι τας δουλας μου; cf. Joel 3 2 in Th (p. 1653 A), while in Cy (p. 376 C) the second μου is missing.

Heb 10 38: ο δε δικαιος μου εκ πιστεως ζησεται; cf. Hab 2 4 according to Th (p. 1820 B); in Cy (p. 869 D) μου is missing.

John 19 37: οψονται εις ον εξεκεντησαν; cf. Zech 12 10 in Th (p. 1945 A); Cy (p. 221–3) offers here: επι βλεψονται...κατωρχησαντο. See the discussion of this passage above III a 5.

In these five instances the quotations of the NT are the actual textual readings of Theodoret. This is in keeping with our statement at the end of XV that Theodoret's text belongs basically to the asterisk type. Of course we do not assume that the text preserved these characteristics throughout; the following example (*I could find no more*) will show a confusion of the readings, suggestive of an already mixed type of these texts:

Acts 2 19: και δωσω τερατα εν τω ουρανω ανω και σημεια επι της γης κατω; cf. Joel 3 3 in Cy (p. 381 C); in Th (p. 1653 C) the words ανω, σημεια and κατω are missing.

3. *OT quotations in the NT and the Vetus Latina.*

Matth 15 7, 8 and similarly Mark 7 6: ο λαος ουτος τοις χειλεσι με τιμα; cf. Is 29 13 according to B: ο λαος ουτος ... εν τοις χειλεσιν αυτων τιμωσιν με. The main difference lies in the treatment of the collective noun λαος as a singular (τιμα in the NT passages), or as a plural (τιμωσιν in B, corresponding to MT כבדוני). The same difference is reflected in the two Old Latin translations of this verse in Is; cf. Ranke, p. 261: honorant me (pl.) — glorificat me (sing.).

Phil 2 10, 11: ινα εν τω ονοματι ιησου παν γονυ καμψη ... και πασα γλωσσα εξομολογησεται. These phrases are borrowed from Is 45 23, a passage which reads in B: οτι εμοι καμψει παν γονυ και ομειται πασα γλωσσα. These two readings εξομολογησεται and ομειται are combined into a doublet in one tradition within the Vetus Latina; cf. Ranke, p. 265: et iurauit omnis lingua (=B) — et iurabit et confitebitur omnis lingua (=B and NT).

Matth 9 13, 12 7: ελεος θελω και ου θυσιαν; cf. Hos 6 6 in B: ελεος θελω η θυσιαν. Similarly Ranke, p. 253: misericordiam uolo quam sacrificium (=B) — misericordiam volo et non sacrificium (=NT).

In these three instances we are fortunate to have parallel evidence from two Old Latin translations; the fact in itself that they reflect a Greek Bible text according to the NT and the LXX, respectively, proves them to be independent translations, without any inner interdependence.

I Cor 5 13: εξαρατε τον πονηρον εξ υμων αυτων is obviously a quotation from Dt 17 7; cf. B: εξαρεις τον πονηρον εξ υμων αυτων. The plural form of the verb εξαρατε (NT) is evidenced by: auferetis malignum ex uobis ipsis (Ulysse Robert, *Heptateuchi Versio Latina Antiquissima*, Lyon 1900, 13).

Acts 7 30: ωφθη αυτω ... αγγελος κυριου εν φλογι πυρος; this narrative is based upon Ex 3 2, which reads in B: ωφθη δε αυτω αγγελος κυριου εν πυρι φλογος. The word-order and construction of this verse according to the NT are corroborated in the Old Latin translation: paruit autem ei angelus domini *in flamma ignis* (Ulysse Robert, *Pentateuchi Versio Latina Antiquissima*, Paris 1881, 167).

In chapter V we stated that the aim of this study was to identify the "Bible of the Apostles"; cf. our definition of this term there. Summing up the results of our discussion in this chapter we may now say that *the "Bible of the Apostles" is identical with the asterisk type of the Hexaplaric LXX*, which thus antedates by centuries the days of Origen.

XVIII. THE FINAL REDACTION OF THE HEBREW BIBLE.

In the MT of the Hebrew Bible the history of the Kingdom of Judah and the House of David is narrated twice: in the Former Prophets (from 1 Sam 31 on) and in Chronicles (from 1 Chron 10 on). We entirely disregard here those paraphrases and other additions of the respective redactors; they are meant to form the "prophetic" background for the narrative of historic events, and reflect in their language and ideology the relatively late period of the compilers of these books. We must concern ourselves solely with the approximately 470 verses of strictly historic character, which we would call the *Annales*, and which are included in almost the identical wording in these two sources. With the slight differences, which show that they are *two recensions of one original*, and which are either differences in dialect (cf. *TRL*, paragraph XXXIII) — including differences in the vocabulary, morphology and syntax — or merely the result of scribal errors, I have dealt exhaustively in *HPT*, by grouping and classifying them together with related source-material. Here I should like to take up another aspect of this problem. Since these *Annales* are common to both historic sources (the Former Prophets and Chronicles), can we still trace any indication of the period when the one recension was finally assigned to the Former Prophets, while the other was incorporated in Chronicles? In other words: can we fix an approximate date for the final redaction of these Biblical books? Here, too,

Origen's *Hexapla* proves very helpful, as the following items will demonstrate. I derive the material from quotations of passages of the Former Prophets which have their parallel in Chronicles, and vice versa; while quoting *one* historic book, Origen's quotation reflects not the recension of this book, but that of the other book. This clearly points to the fact that at the time when Origen's sources, the asterisk and the obelus texts, were composed, a time which may of course have been considerably earlier than his own, the two recensions of the *Annales* were not yet finally assigned to the respective Biblical book; the final redaction of these books must have taken place at a later period.

A. O′ REFLECTS THE PARALLEL TEXT INSTEAD OF MT.

I. O′ offers a translation of the variant Parallel Text.

§ 1. NO EVIDENCE IS PRESERVED OF A TRANSLATION OF MT.

a. *O′ on the Former Prophets.*

2 Sam 10 6: בדוד: O′: ο λαος δαυιδ. The translator had before him 1 Chron 19 6: עִם דָּוִיד, which he read: עַם דוִיד. This difference in the pronunciation is explained by the fact that the Hebrew Bible at that early period consisted of consonants only, without vowel signs, cf. *TRL*, paragraph XV. .

2 Sam 5 23: הסב אל אחריהם: O′: αποστρεφου απ αυτων. Cf. 1 Chron 14 14: הסב מעליהם.

2 Sam 8 13: כהנים היו: O′: αυλαρχαι ησαν. Cf. 1 Chron 18 17: הראשנים ליד המלך.

b. *O′ on Chronicles.*

1 Chron 11 1: ויקבצו: O′: και ηλθε. Cf. 2 Sam 5 1: ויבאו.

1 Chron 17 5: מאהל אל אהל: O′: εν σκηνη. Cf. 2 Sam 7 6: באהל. For an explanation of the Hebrew variant see *HPT* § 12.

1 Chron 17 5: וממשכן: O′: και εν καλυμματι. Cf. 2 Sam 7 6: ובמשכן; see also *HPT*, § 12.

1 Chron 17 6: שפטי: O': φυλην. Cf. 2 Sam 7 7: שבטי. See also
HPT, § 13. Similarly cf. Micah 4 14: שפט, which appears
in Cyril of Alexandria's commentary as φυλας, and which in
turn was misunderstood by codex B for πυλας (*JBL*, 1935,
81).

1 Chron 21 20: את המלאך. O' τον βασιλεα. Cf. 2 Sam 24 20: את המלך.
See also *HPT*, § 38 a, especially the instance from 2 Sam
11 1 — 1 Chron 20 1.

§ 2. UNDER AL EX MT IS GIVEN.

a. *O' on the Former Prophets.*

2 Sam 6 11: את עבד אדם ואת כל ביתו: O': ολον τον οικον αβεδδαρα
και παντα τα αυτου; al ex: τον αβεδδαρα και ολον τον οικον
αυτου. On O' cf. 1 Chron 13 4: את בית עבד אדם ואת כל אשר לו.
Thus, ολον remains without a corresponding equivalent in
the Hebrew text. Whether the translator really had את כל
בית before him, or whether ολον was merely inserted under
the influence of the following παντα, remains in doubt.
On ολος as equivalent to כל cf. Dt 6 22: ובכל ביתו: O': και
εν ※ ολω ✗ τω οικω αυτου.

2 Sam 7 21: בעבור דברך: O': και δια τον δουλον σου; al ex: δια
τον λογον σου. On O' cf. 1 Chron 17 19: בעבור עבדך.

1 Kg 10 29: מרכבה ממצרים: O': εξ αιγυπτου αρμα; al ex: αρματα
εξ αιγυπτου. On O' cf. 2 Chron 1 17: ממצרים מרכבה; see also
HPT, § 121, 10. The difference in the interpretation of
מרכבה as a singular or plural reflects a similar divergent
conception of collective nouns in the Hebrew text, cf.
HPT, § 91.

b. *O' on Chronicles.*

1 Chron 10 1: וינס: O': και εφυγον; al ex: και εφυγεν. On O' cf.
1 Sam 31 1: וינסו; see also *HPT*, § 92 and note 313 there.

1 Chron 11 4: דויד וכל ישראל: O': ο βασιλευς και ανδρες αυτου; al
ex: ο βασιλευς δαυιδ και πας ισραηλ. On O' cf. 2 Sam 5 6:
המלך ואנשיו; al ex reflect a combination of both reports: המלך//
דויד; cf. similar cases of doublets under c.

1 Chron 11 5: ויאמרו ישבי יבוס לדויד: O': ειπαν τω δαυιδ; al ex: ειπαν δε οι κατοικουντες την ιηβους τω δαυιδ. On O' cf. 2 Sam 5 6: ויאמר לדוד; see also *HPT*, § 122 a.

1 Chron 11 23: מדה: O': ορατον; al ex: ευμηκη. On O' cf. 2 Sam 23 21: מראה: see also *HPT*, § 21.

1 Chron 14 7: ובעלידע: O': και ελιαδε; al ex: και βααλιαδα. On O' cf. 2 Sam 5 16: ואלידע.

1 Chron 17 14: והעמדתיהו: O': και πιστωσω αυτον; al ex: και στησω αυτον. On O' cf. 2 Sam 7 16: ונאמן.

1 Chron 17 21: הלך: O': ωδηγησεν αυτον; al ex: επορευθη. On O' cf. 2 Sam 7 23: הָלְכוּ, read as הֹלְכוֹ; on the change in the pronunciation involved cf. above in § 1 a the instance from 2 Sam 10 6.

2 Chron 13 2: מיכיהו: O': μααχα; al ex: μιχαια. On O' cf. 1 Kg 15 2: מעכה.

2 Chron 15 16: אם אסא המלך: O': την μητερα αυτου; al ex: την μητερα ασα του βασιλεως. On O' cf. 1 Kg 15 13: אמו.

c. *Doublets.*

2 Sam 6 2: להעלות: O': εν αναβασει // του αναγαγειν. The first translation corresponds to 1 Chron 13 6: בַּעֲלָתָה, interpreted as בַּעֲלִיָתָה, cf. *HPT*, note 441; του αναγαγειν = MT.

2 Chron 5 9: מן הארון: O': εκ των αγιων; al ex: απο της κιβωτου // εκ των αγιων. On O' cf. 1 Kg 8 8: מן הקדש; al ex combines this reading with MT; cf. above in b the instance from 1 Chron 11 4.

II. O' omits words and phrases of MT, which are not included in the Parallel Text.

§ 3. *Sub asterisco* MT is given.

2 Sam 8 14: שם נצבים: O': Vacat. ※ εθηκεν εστηλωμενους ✗. Cf. 1 Chron 18 13.

1 Kg 12 16: דבר: O': ※ λογον ✗. Cf. 2 Chron 10 16; for an explanation of the Hebrew insertion see *HPT*, § 124 a 1.

1 Kg 14 31: ושם אמו נעמה העמנית: O': Vacat. ※ και ονομα της μητρος αυτου νααμα η αμμανιτις ✗. Cf. 2 Chron 12 13.

1 Kg 22 4: אל מלך ישראל: O': Vacat. ※ προς βασιλεα ισραηλ ⋎.
Cf. 2 Chron 18 3.

1 Kg 22 15: אליו: O': ※ προς αυτον ⋎. Cf. 2 Chron 18 14; see also
HPT, § 117 c.

2 Kg 8 19: לו: O': ※ αυτω ⋎. Cf. 2 Chron 21 7; see also *HPT*,
§ 117 c.

2 Kg 8 29: ארמים: O': ※ οι συροι ⋎. Cf. 2 Chron 22 6; see also
HPT, § 122 a.

2 Kg 11 17: ובין העם (2°): O': ※ και αναμεσον του βασιλεως και αναμεσον του λαου ⋎. Cf. 2 Chron 23 16. The Hebrew
text of this Kg-passage offers an obvious doublet. Further
instances for identifying Hebrew doublets by means of
asterisk quotations in Origen, cf. 2 Sam 6 3–4: וישאהו מבית
אבינדב אשר בגבעה; Dt 17 5: או את האשה... אשר עשו ;1 Kg 2 5:
לו חות יאיר בן מנשה אשר בגלעד ib. 4 13: בשלום ויתן דמי מלחמה;
ib. 5 4: מתפסח ועד עזה בכל מלכי עבר הנהר. The O'-translations
of these passages are quoted *sub asterisco* in Field's *Hexapla*.

2 Kg 15 34: עשה (2°): O': ※ εποιησεν ⋎. Cf. 2 Chron 27 2.

§ 4. Under al ex MT is given.

1 Sam 31 11: אליו: O': Vacat. al ex: περι αυτου. On O' cf. 1 Chron
10 11.

1 Kg 12 15: דבר יהוה: O': ελαλησεν; al ex: ελαλησεν κυριος. On O'
cf. 2 Chron 10 15.

1 Chron 13 14: בביתו: O': Vacat. al ex: εν τω οικω αυτου. On O'
cf. 2 Sam 6 11.

1 Chron 13 14: את בית עבד אדם: O': αβεδδαρα; al ex: τον οικον
αβεδδαρα. On O' cf. 2 Sam 6 11.

B. O' TRANSLATES MT, BUT AL EX THE PARALLEL TEXT.

a. *O' on the Former Prophets.*

2 Sam 5 21: ואנשיו: O': και οι ανδρες οι μετ αυτου; al ex: και οι
ανδρες αυτου. και ειπε κατακαυσαι αυτους εν πυρι. On al ex
cf. 1 Chron 14 12: **ויאמר דוד וישרפו באש**; on the difference
between the passive construction of the Hebrew verb in
Chron and its active form in al ex, cf. *HPT*, § 61 a a.

2 Sam 10 8: פתח השער: O': παρα τη θυρα της πυλης; al ex: παρα του πυλωνα της πολεως. On al ex cf. 1 Chron 19 9: פתח העיר.

2 Sam 12 31: וישם: O': και εθηκεν; al ex: και διεπρισεν. On al ex cf. 1 Chron 20 3: וישר; see also *HPT*, § 19.

2 Sam 23 13: אל קציר: O': εις κασων; al ex: εις την πετραν. On al ex cf. 1 Chron 11 15. The rendering εις seems to reflect a Hebrew preposition אל; on the interchangeability of על and אל in Hebrew, cf. *HPT*, § 120. O' transliterates the ר in קציר with N (in κασων), cf. *HPT*, § 19.

2 Sam 24 10: אשר עשיתי: O': ο εποιησα; al ex: ποιησας το ρημα τουτο. On al ex cf. 1 Chron 21 8: הזה הדבר את עשיתי אשר.

2 Sam 24 17: אנכי חטאתי ואנכי העויתי: O': εγω ειμι ηδικησα; al ex: εγω ημαρτηκα και εγω ειμι ο ποιμην εκακοποιησα. On al ex cf. 1 Chron 21 17: וְהָרֵעַ הֲרֵעֹתִי, translated as: וְהָרֹעָה הֲרֵעֹתִי, with dittography of the ה, cf. *HPT*, § 35 β. As to the difference in the pronunciation of the word in question, cf. our remark on 2 Sam 10 6 above in § 1 a. On the difficulty of the Greek construction under O': ειμι with a verb in the aorist tense (ηδικησα), cf. X, § 5 d, and the cross-references marked there.

b. *O' on Chronicles.*

1 Chron 10 11: יבש גלעד: O': οι κατοικουντες γαλααδ; al ex: οι κατοικουντες ιαβις της γαλααδ. On al ex cf. 1 Sam 31 11: ישבי יביש גלעד. Under O' the Hebrew יבש is obviously translated as ישב or ישבי, cf. *HPT*, § 91. On metathesis in the Hebrew Bible see *HPT*, § 36.

1 Chron 11 13: שעורים: O': κριθων; al ex: φακου. On al ex cf. 2 Sam 23 11: עדשים. The interrelation between these two Hebrew readings is explained in *HPT*, § 36 β.

1 Chron 13 6: שם: O': ονομα αυτου; al ex: ονομα αυτου εκει. On al ex cf. 2 Sam 6 2: שָׁם שֵׁם, read here as: שָׁם שָׁם. As to the change in the pronunciation, cf. our remark on 2 Sam 10 6 above § 1 a.

1 Chron 18 2: ויהיו: O': και ησαν; al ex: και εγενηθη. On the singular in al ex cf. 2 Sam 8 2: ותהי. For the difference in the gender of these Hebrew verbal forms, see *HPT*, § 88 γ.
2 Chron 6 9: כי: O': οτι; al ex: αλλ η. On al ex cf. 1 Kg 8 19: כי אם; see also *HPT*, § 124 b 3.
2 Chron 7 7: ואת החלבים: O': και τα στεατα; al ex: και τα στεατα των ειρηνικων. On al ex cf. 1 Kg 8 64: ואת חלבי השלמים.
2 Chron 13 2: בת אוריאל מן גבעה: O': θυγατηρ ουριηλ απο γαβαων; ai ex θυγατηρ αβεσσαλωμ. On al ex cf. 1 Kg 15 2: בת אבשלום.

INDEX OF PASSAGES FROM THE OT AND NT WHICH ARE
QUOTED HERE IN GREEK OR LATIN:

Genesis		44 28	224	14 26	212	28 30	251, 253
		45 3	232	15 4	228, 250	32	250
1 14	242	46 8	212	16	212	33	253, 254
2 9	253	21	212	18	254	34	253
3 6	251	47 5	214	25	252	29 28	251
14	251	48 16	253	16 4	230	42	253
4 8	242	49 6	254	10	221	30 8	225, 253
15	252	7	254	18 1	236	10	229
8 9	255	50 5	221	7	246	32 24	278
13 14	252	18	219	14	254	33 2	243
15 11	235, 251			19 21	253	5	229, 250
13	254	Exodus		20 18	217	6	254
16 6	254			21 8	215	16	253
9	254	1 9	253	22 4	242	19	276
18 1	236	19	252	9	253	34 7	278
10	251	2 6	219	12	230	11	243
19 38	252	3 2	220, 277	16	254	15	251
20 4	229, 250		282	23 18	240	35 6	253
10	254	4	221	28	239	22	243
21 22	251	4 6	242	25 4	253		
22 13	252	10	241	17	228, 250	Leviticus	
23 13	251	6 7	254	23	256	1 3	232
16	251	13	239	24	235	8	251
24 5	250	16	211	25	228	4 7	240
39	250	22	239	26 1	253	25	233
26 29	252	8 2	256	3	255	5 19	276
27 45	254	5	242	5	256	7 3	256
28 8	230	9 16	254, 280	6	255	8 5	254
18	252	18	251	12	255	9 4	240
20	253	24	212	13	225, 251	11 42	251
29 12	247	10 4	252	16	242	13 2	224
30 15	252	5	252	31	253	4	224
32 14	246	6	255	27 20	228, 252	13	256
33 1	246	11 3	219		253	37	256
34 21	246	12 5	231	28 3	225	14 48	252
37 14	254	40	242	6	253	15 1	250
38 1	251, 253	41	212	8	253	16 31	225
39 19	254	46	199	15	253	17 3, 4	255
41 56	255	14 7	250	20	256	19 20	243
44 18	251	10	221				

22 15 241
18 230
21 247
23 40 254
25 45 225, 253
26 16 230
22 252
27 18 253

Numbers

1 44 243
53 215
2 3 230
7 220
3 15 214, 229
17 211
51 217
5 8 255
6 3 231
7 251
19 212
10 31 212
34 212
35 232
12 12 228
13 10 211
14 22, 23 245
15 6 234
11 233
19 235, 251
20 251
16 3 239
17 2 229
6 215
21 5 212
22 23 212
25 15 252
26 62 212
27 14 252
28 6 253
13 217
23 256
30 11 216
33 2 216
34 29 241

Deuteron.

1 7 246
8 212
2 5 246
3 17 236
24 254
4 16 221
20 256
5 7 211
6 15 221
22 285
7 1 224, 239
15 229
25 221
8 4 254
9 26 214
28 243
10 11 243
13 18 224
14 8 243
15 3 220
8 230, 247
21 230
17 5 287
7 282
18 5 243
19 14 211
21 9 214
22 17 241
23 10 241
24 14 240
27 20 211
28 27 240
66 241
29 2 253
31 5 233, 241
6 225, 253
32 35 232
43 240

Joshua

1 7 233
4 10 216
5 6 227
6 5 233
26 244
8 2 216
9 4 228
24 247
10 11 234
11 14 247
12 2 215
4 216
16 10 244
17 11 213
19 17 213
22 213
30 213
32 214
38 213
20 3 245
21 43 254
22 16 247

Judges

1 1 260, 262, 263
2 263
3 260, 263
4 263
5 263
6 261, 262
7 261, 262
8 262, 263
9 262, 263
10 227, 260, 261
11 226, 260, 262
12 262, 263
14 234, 260
16 260
17 228, 260
20 228
23 227
27 228
36 218
2 10 261
17 261
3 7 261
8 217
16 261
4 9 247
5 8 227
10 232
29 230
8 11 231
33 231
9 4 224
46 231
54 247
11 34 230
13 2 226
15 5 226
16 16 232
18 2 226
11 226
20 13 227
15 228
21 19 228

1 Samuel

1 1 264
3 264
4 264
9 265
11 265
13 265
16 232
7 4 226
12 226
9 21 226
10 19 226
20 226
14 47 234
15 8 226
32 231
33 231
16 14 232
20 9 247
35 227
21 8 226
23 14 226
19 226

24 23	226	2 Kings		23 22	278	11 1	197
31 11	287			27 6	230	13 3	264, 269
		1 3	224	31 15	198		
2 Samuel		9	230	33 9	217, 221	Joel	
		2 18	219	34 5	226		
1 19	225	8 19	287	35 18	220	3 2	281
25	225	29	287	36 6	220	3	281
3 27	232	11 17	287	43 6	227		
5 21	287	14 10	229	46 20	233	Amos	
23	284	15 34	287	48 13	225		
6 2	286	16 18	229	49 3	230	6 2	270
3, 4	287	19 16	248	22	233	8	248
11	285			51 34	235		
7 21	285	Isaiah		52 7	227	Obadiah	
8 14	286						
18	284	1 27	233			16	269
10 6	284	2 5	232	Ezekiel			
8	288	3 2	228			Micah	
12 31	288	23	228	3 5	264		
19 8	235	5 1	227	9	265	4 14	285
23 13	288	9 5	234	18	266	5 1	196
24 10	288	14 2	227	4 2	266	3	229
17	288	8	231	6 9	265		
		9	230	21 24, 25	230	Nahum	
1 Kings		15 6	233	24 9	277		
		24 8	227	18	220	3 12	270
2 5	287	14	227	27 19	220		
4 13	287	28 16	201, 280	34 16	277	Hab	
5 4	287	29 7	277	27	277		
32	219	13	277, 282			2 4	281
6 1	229	40 4	280	Hosea		3 12	269
8 64	219	13	227				
9 9	219	42 1	280	1 2	264, 277	Zeph	
10 29	285	1–4	198	4	266		
12 15	287	45 23	282	7	264	1 5	270
16	219, 286	51 23	229	2 25	264		
14 31	286	53 12	253	4 4	266	Zech	
17 22	219	59 8	280	5	266		
18 39	219	66 7	228	19	270, 275	6 7	270
43	219			5 13	266	7 3	270
44	232	Jeremia		6 4	277	12 10	199, 281
19 18	280			6	201, 264	13 5	248
21 29	247	5 15	227		277, 280	7	281
22 4	287	15 1	218		281, 282	Psalms	
15	287	18 6	277	8 1	269		
38	225	22 14	278	9 10	270	103 2	265
		28	277	10 8	281	104 4	252

104 18 **211, 265**	2 20 **228**	Matthew		Acts
25 **246**	22 **232, 233**	2 4, 6 **196**		2 16, 18 **281**
116 16 **247**	3 23 **277**	14, 15 **197**		19 **281**
118 10 **247**	5 10 **228**	17, 18 **197**		7 30 **277, 282**
		9 13 **201, 280**		17 2, 3 **194**
Prov	1 Chron	**281, 282**		11 **195**
3 12 **280**	10 1 **285**	12 7 **201, 280 281**		1 Peter
Ruth	11 **288**	17, 18 **280**		
	11 1 **284**	17—21 **198**		2 3–6 **202**
1 1 **275, 276**	4 **285**	15 7, 8 **282**		
2 **273**	5 **286**	22 37 **223**		Rom
5 **275**	13 **288**	26 31 **281**		
11 **273**	23 **286**			3 16, 17 **280**
14 **273**	13 6 **229, 288**			9 17 **254, 280**
16 **274**	14 **287**	Mark		21 **277**
22 **276**	14 7 **286**			33 **201, 280**
2 13 **221**	17 5 **284**	7 6 **282**		11 4 **280**
16 **225**	6 **285**	12 30 **223**		
21 **273**	14 **286**			1 Cor
22 **276**	21 **286**	Luke		2 16 **227**
23 **276**	18 2 **289**			5 13 **282**
3 7 **276**	21 20 **285**	3 4, 5 **280**		
10 **273**		10 27 **223**		Phil
15 **275**	2 Chron	22 37 **253**		
16 **275**		23 30 **281**		2 10, 11 **282**
	5 9 **286**			
Threni	6 9 **289**	John		Heb
	7 7 **289**			1 7 **252**
1 12 **235**	13 2 **286, 289**	19 32—37 **199,**		10 38 **281**
2 16 **220**	15 16 **286**	**281**		12 6 **280**

www.ingramcontent.com/pod-product-compliance
Lightning Source LLC
Chambersburg PA
CBHW070302100426
42743CB00011B/2315